THE
ROMAN COMMONWEALTH

Frontispiece.

PLATE I.—RELIEF FROM THE ARA PACIS, ROME.

The scene is of a public sacrifice on a State occasion. The central figure is probably that of the Pontifex Maximus (Lepidus): on the right is probably Julia, daughter of Augustus, the little boy her son Lucius Caesar; on her right is her

THE ROMAN
COMMONWEALTH

By

R. W. MOORE

HEAD MASTER OF HARROW SCHOOL

KENNIKAT PRESS
Port Washington, N. Y./London

THE ROMAN COMMONWEALTH

First published in 1942
Reissued in 1969 by Kennikat Press
Library of Congress Catalog Card No: 72-101048
SBN 8046-0713-3

Manufactured by Taylor Publishing Company   Dallas, Texas

KENNIKAT CLASSICS SERIES

CONIVGI
AMANTISSIMAE

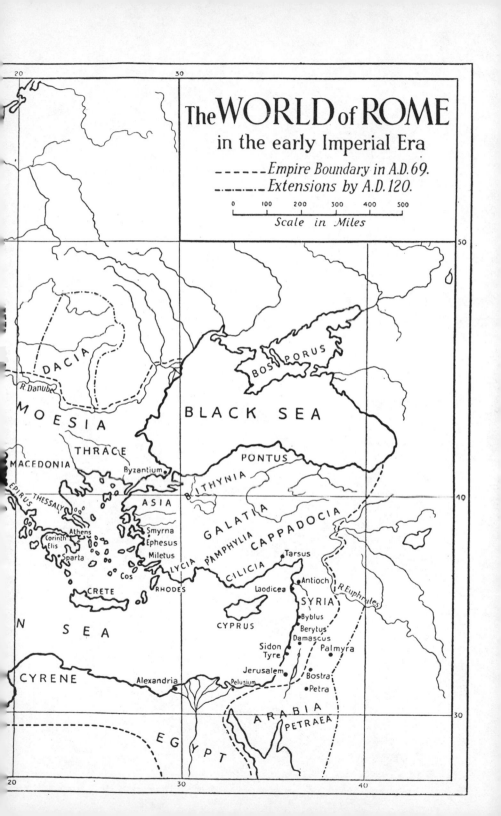

PREFACE

IN this book I have tried to give an account of Roman culture and Roman life as it was in its prime. I have tried to explain that culture and to describe that life in such a way as to answer the questions which might be asked by an interested modern who, constantly meeting references to Rome and vaguely aware of its importance, wished to see a coherent picture and to know what it was all about. However fragmentary and haphazard his knowledge of the ancient world may be, he cannot escape the fact that in institutions and idioms, in ways of thought and in ways of action, our Western world is for ever reflecting a Roman past. It is in our speech; it is in our buildings; it is in the bundles of device we call government; it is in our literature and it is in our law. Of the 20,000 words most commonly used in ordinary written English over 10,000 are Latin. The vocabulary of politics, government and law is almost entirely Latin: *liberal, conservative, propaganda, committee, statute, legislation, territory, aggression, conciliation, offence, referendum, pact*—an endless stream immediately suggests itself. And there are the more colourful words and the words that tell a tale—*gladiator, family, plebiscite, consul, prefect, legion, fascist, majesty, dominion*, to mention but a few. There are many words, too, indispensable for the expression of our ideals in society and service which we cannot understand to the full without going back in thought to the world which gave them birth: *industry, diligence, continence, gravity, dignity,* even *virtue* itself. In these no less than in the imposing monuments which Rome has left us—the roads, the walls, the bridges, aqueducts, triumphal archways, basilicas—the Roman genius for the practicalities of civilized life is implicit and compelling. In an age which in the meteoric progress of scientific invention has left behind the economies of the ancient world the ways of the ancients are in danger of being forgotten. But the ancients were the pioneers and they laid the foundations of the world we know today. Without some knowledge of them we are intellectually without root. To disregard them is to disregard the most significant scientific principle of our age, the principle of evolution.

Two further observations must be made by way of preface. The first relates to the space which the reader will find devoted to a consideration of Greek things in a book about Rome; the second would anticipate the criticism which will be directed against the book on the ground that it is a picture seen through rose-coloured spectacles. On the first point it may be observed that it is an essential part of our debt to Rome that she preserved for us so much of the Greek culture. The world of Greece in time runs into the world of Rome, so much so that it is hard to separate them, nor would such a separation be of great value. It is then no disproportion or distraction to subsume at certain points the Greek culture under the Roman. For we are taking the section of a world. On the second point it must be made clear that this book does not primarily aim at the realism which dwells on the seamy side of the picture. That province can be safely left to the novelists and moralists, of whom there is no lack (some of their names may be found in the Book List at the end of the book). There is no doubt that the ancient world was largely vitiated by the institution of slavery, which was fatal to morality and invention alike. There is no denying that much of the Roman story is a dismal and bloody chronicle of blindness, cruelty and failure. So are the stories of most nations. But that is not all. Out of that history was born much that has lived to quicken our progress. And looking back from the present to the past and sorting the immortal from the transient, the quick parts from the dead, we can discard much. The sickening side of Juvenal and Tacitus may not be irrelevant, but life is short, and these are not the things that count. The same may be said of the conventional condemnatory attitude to Rome of the Decline and Fall, but I have more to say on this elsewhere.

For the rest, the book is frankly eclectic and introductory. It will not be difficult to find omissions and curtailments, half-treatments and slurrings-over. For these I can make only the present apology, trusting that the rough sketch will not be taken for the finished portrait. For the portrait of Rome is a consummation reached only in the mind after patient study, a study in which there is much profit and much delight. The reader who may wish to pursue it will find guidance in the list of books, to which, among others, I owe a debt too various and of too long standing to be defined.

I wish to thank Mr. R. Meiggs of Balliol College,

Oxford, and Mr. F. W. King of Winchester College for their kindness in reading proofs and for many valuable suggestions (they are in no way responsible for any blemishes that remain); the Delegates of the Clarendon Press for permission to reprint sections of the book which have previously appeared in " Greece and Rome "; Mr. Raymond Savage and the Lawrence Trustees for permission to quote from the published letters of T. E. Lawrence the passage which appears on page 229 ; and my wife for unfailing help in all stages of the book's making.

R. W. M.

BRISTOL, 1942.

CONTENTS

ILLUSTRATIONS

ACKNOWLEDGMENTS

THE author's and publishers' grateful acknowledgments are due to Dr. R. C. Carrington and the Clarendon Press for the line diagrams in the text; and for copyright photographs and permission for reproductions as set out below.

PLATE

I. From *Roman Art*, by A. W. Seaby. B. T. Batsford, Ltd.

II. Photos: British Museum.

III. Photos: British Museum.

IV. Photo: British Museum.

V. Photos: British Museum.

VI. Photo: British Museum.

VII. From *Greece and Rome*, Vol. V. Clarendon Press. Photo: Provinzialmuseum Trier.

VIII. From *History of Rome*, by C. E. Robinson. Methuen & Co., Ltd. Photo: Alinari.

IX. (1) From *History of Rome*, by C. E. Robinson. Methuen & Co., Ltd. Photo: Anderson.

(2) Photo: The Times Publishing Co. Ltd.

X. From *Life of Rome*, by Rogers and Harley. Clarendon Press.

XI. From *Pompeii*, by R. C. Carrington. Clarendon Press. Photo: Anderson.

XII. From *Pompeii*, by R. C. Carrington. Clarendon Press.

XIII. From *Pompeii*, by R. C. Carrington. Clarendon Press.

XIV. (1) Photo: Author.
(2) Photo: Professor C. Calza and Sig. I. Gismondi. Clarendon Press.

XV. Photo: R.A.F. Official: Crown Copyright Reserved.

XVI. Photos: Author.

XVII. Photos: Author.

XVIII. From *The Ancient World*, by J. M. Todd.

XIX. From *History of Rome*, by C. E. Robinson. Methuen & Co., Ltd.

XX. From *History of Rome*, by C. E. Robinson. Methuen & Co., Ltd. Photo: Boissones.

XXI. From *History of Rome*, by C. E. Robinson. Methuen & Co., Ltd. Photo: Boissones.

XXII. Photo: Gibson & Son, Hexham.

XXIII. From *Roman Britain*, by R. G. Collingwood. Clarendon Press.

XXIV. Photo: Journal of Roman Studies.

CHAPTER I

ROMAN BEGINNINGS

Non sine causa dii hominesque hunc urbi condendae locum elegerunt . . . ad incrementum urbis natum unice locum.—LIVY.

" Not for nothing did god and man conspire to choose this place to make a city . . . a site without rival for a city which is to grow."

OGNI strada men'a Roma: all roads, it has been said, lead to Rome. However the saying may have been primarily intended, it has for the historian undeniable truth. There is so much in the world of history which, germinating from Rome, can be traced back with certainty to its root. We owe to Rome the greater part of the framework of our civilization, our law, our constitutions, methods of holding people together in orderly societies and much of the apparatus which has been found useful to this end; and beyond the material legacy there is a spiritual: certain ways of looking at life, certain ideals of efficiency and service.

It is a commonplace to acknowledge the debt which our Western world owes to the mind of the Greek, to the spiritual intensity of the Jew and to the Roman as the man of affairs; and the distinctions implied are substantially true, so long as we do not deny the Roman a mind and an inspiration. The practical intelligence of the Roman was a genius, and the important thing about his culture is not the machinery he invented but the sense of order which prompted the invention. Rightly we look to the Greeks to find the source of creative ideas in art, the sciences and speculative thought, but we must

15

not deny the term " creative " to those political ideas which had their birth in Rome or forget that it was the Roman genius which preserved the fruits of the Greek genius for the modern world. The two are inseparable; simplification may be falsification, but it is still substantially true that Rome applied what Greece thought out. The New Testament was written in Greek, but it was the Roman peace which made possible the spreading of the Word, and that is not all. The genius of Christendom is as much Latin as Greek. In the *Aeneid* of Virgil, in Augustine's *City of God*, in the *Divine Comedy* of Dante we have visions seen positively in the idiom of Rome. No sooner has Rome ceased to rule a world-empire than she becomes the head of a world-church.

All roads lead to Rome, and we can all find our way to Rome on the map. And, seeing how many times Rome has survived events which other capitals of the world—Nineveh, Babylon, Athens—have found fatal, Rome, we say, is eternal. But Rome was not always on the map. Perhaps if she had been she could hardly have found her way to the best place on it. Nor was she always the many-sided thing we have found her to be. She grew slowly from humble beginnings, and we cannot appreciate her ultimate stature unless we watch the process of her growth. Compared with the life of this slow and deliberate child, the career of the Greeks was meteoric. Athens, like her patron goddess, seems to spring almost fully-fledged from the head of Zeus. Within two generations she had sprung into the most vital centre of art and thought the world has known and in the same brilliant career had begun to found an empire; but within a few years the vitality was gone. Alexander conquered the world from the Aegean to the

PLATE II.—ROMAN PORTRAIT BUSTS.

1. A young Roman countryman. 2. A Roman lady (Julia Mamaea).

Indus; but he too died young, and his brave new world hardly survived him. The Roman was a backward child but sturdy; he started without promise, made mistake after mistake, but there was something inside him that made him go on, and his world survived.

The map of Italy shows us a long narrow peninsula, some three-quarters mountain. But it slopes west. The spinal cord of the Apennines is much closer to the east coast, where it descends steeply to the sea, than to the west; and on the west there are fertile valleys running up into the hills and rivers watering coastal plains. These plains are alluvial. Their fertility is largely due to the deposits from the widespread volcanic action to which in early times the coastal region was subject. This volcanic action may help to explain why the district of Campania and Etruria was left comparatively unpeopled when neolithic man was settling in most other parts of the peninsula. A district disturbed by constant volcanic eruptions is no place to live in. However that may be, Italy seen from the west and north is a beautiful country and invites the newcomer. In the north the lush green Lombardy plain unfolds itself across to the Venice flats and a misty sea-horizon; down the west coast the plains of Etruria and Campania are but the prelude to the sun-drenched, wider plains beyond; and always there are the mountains affording a sharp contrast and upland pastures for the farmer. It is a land of fruitful vegetation, of oliveyards and vine-clad slopes, of sharp, commanding contours and soft filling, of a brilliance which lights up the whole from the gaunt mountain sinews to the far-spread silver-blue sea. " Tell me, all you who have journeyed through many

2

lands, have you seen a richer-tilled land than Italy ? "
asks the Roman writer Varro, and he was no facile
enthusiast or propagandist but a sober encyclopaedist.

This is not the place to inquire into its ethnographical
history. It will be enough to say that its historic peoples, the various Italian tribes, came for the most part
from beyond the Alps. Attracted by the rich Lombardy
plain, they slowly filtered southwards until all the habitable parts of Italy were occupied. Other settlers, such
as the Etruscans, came from the sea, and by the time
that Roman history begins the Greeks had dotted their
settlements round the toe of Italy and were even creeping
up the shin. Always there were comings and goings;
for Italy is by nature well-adapted to penetration by sea
and land. These immigrations began before the beginning of the Bronze Age and continued into the Iron Age.
In their several districts the tribes of Italy developed
their distinctive cultures until the people of the little hill-
town called Rome rose among them to forge them into
one. The Roman historians would have us believe that
Rome was from the first a power appointed by providence to the special task of civilizing first Italy and then
the world. Archaeology has proved the claim untrue.
In the early pages of her history the barbarian is Rome,
attacking civilizations superior to her own, but shrewd
enough to benefit from them and ultimately transcend-
ing them.

If Rome was destined to unite the several cultural
units of primitive Italy, it is easy to see how her geographical position helped. Communications in Italy
are not easy; it is too long and mountainous. But Rome
is just in the middle and strategically placed. En-
larged mountain torrent though it may seem, the Tiber

is the only considerable river south of the Po. By land
and water Rome had easy outlet to the sea, and her
river-sea communication opened up a way into central
Italy. She was near enough to the sea to use it for her
own purposes, but far enough from the sea to be toler-
ably safe from pirates. During the first thousand years
of her history Rome was never attacked from the sea.
From this position she could control the Latian plain to
the south and the Etruscan plain to the north and
gradually extend her power over the mountain communities to the east and south-east. All this in time
she did.

First, as head of the league of tribes in the region of
Latium, Rome has to fight against the Etruscan power
on the north of the river. For a time, somewhere in the
sixth century B.C., she falls completely under the foreign
Etruscan domination, and a dynasty of Etruscan kings
rules in Rome. But from her Etruscan masters she
learns arts which she is to turn to good account in her
own career of conquest later on. When she has driven
out her Etruscan kings, she has still to fight for her life.
By the end of the next century the Etruscan power has
waned, and that threat is past, only to bring Rome herself face to face with the very forces which have worn
down Etruria: the Gauls of the north and the Samnites
of the south-east. In 390 B.C. the Gallic raiders actually
took and sacked Rome. Fortunately they did not stay,
and Rome was left to grapple for the next century with
the enemies in the hills, the Volscians, the Sabines, the
Aequi and the more formidable Samnites. There were
three grim Samnite wars, but Rome won in the end, and
by 290 B.C. she is mistress of central Italy. Where she
conquered she knit together by outposts, colonies and

roads. But the conquest of the Samnites now brought her into direct contact with the Greek cities of the south. In 280 the rich merchant city of Tarentum situated just inside the heel of Italy, alarmed by the upstart power in the north, calls in help from Pyrrhus King of Epirus over the Adriatic. Undismayed by initial defeats, Rome hangs on to Pyrrhus until he gives up and returns. The Greek south is now in her hands. From the Arno in the north (for the Po valley is still Gaul) to the straits of Messina in the south, Italy is now Roman.

But this was only a beginning. Across the straits of Messina Sicily is the merest step, and Sicily was a very rich and desirable land. For centuries, as the history of Athens no less than the many Greek Sicilian colonies testifies, it had been the Greek el Dorado, and, more significantly for Rome, it had also attracted the attentions of the great Phoenician commercial power across the Mediterranean in north Africa which went by the name of Carthage. Carthage could no more tolerate an expanding Rome than Rome an active Carthage. If Carthage were allowed to dominate the Straits of Messina, Rome's communications with south Italy and the Adriatic were no longer safe. The First Punic War, an epic of Roman fortitude eclipsed by the still more dogged heroics of the Second Punic War, left Rome with Sicily at her feet and Carthage a sworn enemy to the death. It was Carthage who died, but not before reducing Rome many times over to all but her last gasp. In the middle of the First Punic War Rome tried to turn herself into a sea-power, lost four fleets and yet won. In the Second Punic War, after repeated bunglings and disasters, by sheer obstinacy she kept her brilliant enemy Hannibal from ever completely

getting within her guard and, thanks to the stupidity of
the enemy's government, was able to carry the fight out
of her own country into his and there to win it. That was
in 202 B.C. In the course of this war Rome mastered
Spain, which at the beginning of the war had been a
sphere of Carthaginian influence and the base from
which Hannibal had marched on Italy. Carthage still
survived, defeated but still dangerously near (so thought
the old die-hard statesman Cato, when he could show in
the senate-house at Rome figs grown on Carthaginian
soil and still fresh). Fifty years later Carthage was
brutally annihilated.

But the geographical thread has only begun to un-
ravel. No sooner is the West in her hands than Rome
has to turn to the East. Over the Adriatic were powers,
more formidable than Pyrrhus's, which had been in
league with Carthage during the death-struggle of the
Punic Wars; and, as the map will show, the passage
from the heel of Italy to the Greek mainland can be
made in a single night. The Straits of Otranto, no less
than the Straits of Messina, needed safeguard. War-
weary as she was (and the Second Punic War had brought
many economic and social disturbances in its train),
Rome could have no peace. War was once more
declared, Philip of Macedon was beaten, and Roman
interest was permanently extended to the Balkans too.
This led to war with the kindred kings of Syria, and
long before the end of the second century B.C. Rome
was irretrievably committed in Asia Minor. She had
already in 168 assumed a protectorate over Egypt.
What force it was that led her so inevitably from step
to step it is not easy to say. Her house at home was
badly out of order by this time, and the government

was not happy about the growing responsibilities abroad or about the new machinery which they involved. Her foreign policy was pieced together out of gestures of defiance and fits of hesitation; she lived from hand to mouth, but she still went on. Self-preservation born in the old Latin days when wars were fought across the Tiber or in the hills a few miles away had become self-assertion, and self-assertion a habit. And she was still a young and unreflective nation, hanging together and effective because she was still resolutely " on the make."

Twenty-two years elapsed between the final defeat of Perseus of Macedon and the annexation of his kingdom; but it was annexed in the end, and annexations still went on. The provinces of Macedon and Africa were formed in 146 B.C.; at the same time Greece became a Roman protectorate; in 133 came the province of Asia; in 121, after wars in south Gaul, Gallia Narbonensis (still called Provence, " the Province "), to safeguard the route to Spain which had hitherto been adequately protected by the powerful Greek city of Marseilles. And still wars came thick and fast, some dangerously near; risings of armed slaves, a dragging war against an African prince, an alarming war against invading hordes of Northern barbarians, fighting in Spain, and then, after a serious patch of political discord, a civil war throughout Italy with the Italian allies. As soon as that is over begins the first of a series of wars against the great Eastern king, Mithridates, interrupted by a growing civil strife in Rome, which has ramifications in Spain and elsewhere, and aggravated by Rome's inability to police the Mediterranean. But the age of the great generals has come, and Rome prevails over all her troubles. Sulla puts Mithridates in his place and stems the revolutionary tide at home. Pompey sweeps the seas clear of pirates, destroys Mithridates and in so doing extends Rome's dominion to the Euphrates. Julius Caesar adds Gaul and would, no doubt, have done his best to add Britain and Mesopotamia, had not the constitutional problem by this time swollen to bursting.

Having acquired the world, Rome now, paradoxically enough, began to set her own house in order. This process involved a century of civil faction, three civil wars and inestimable bloodshed. In the course of this process the constitution slowly but surely underwent a decisive revolution, and Rome insensibly reverted to a monarchy. The trouble had been that she had tried to control an Empire with a constitution framed for a parish. When we first meet her in history her soldiers are ordinary working citizens momentarily called from their everyday work, her generals the annual magistrates who must lay down office at the end of the year. It soon becomes manifest that, to conduct the wars which she must inevitably undertake, annual commands and citizen militias were no longer sufficient. It was no longer enough to call a Cincinnatus and his tenants from the plough to the battlefield and to send them back when the fighting was done. Wars after the fourth century were not so obligingly short or so conveniently near. Formidable enemies mean big wars, and big wars mean big armies and big commands; and it was from the big commands that the revolution came.

Until near the end of the second century B.C. only citizens of a certain property qualification were allowed to serve in the legions. It was the great general Marius who, at a moment of military crisis at the end of the

second century B.C., threw open recruiting to all and
sundry and so created what was virtually a professional
army. Though wars came thick and fast, it was not
entirely a professional army, for there was as yet no
standing field-army, and in intervals of peace the soldier
might find himself unemployed. It was similarly due
to the absence of a standing army that when the need
for troops came the general had usually to raise them
for himself. Thus armies became attached to particular
generals, to whom they would look for reward, in the
shape of money-grants or land-allotments, when their
work was done. To conduct her wars Rome had had
to recruit armies which could not be satisfactorily re-
absorbed into the citizen-body and to give generals
power which did not harmonize with the framework of
the little republican régime. Power was in the hands
of the man who had the legions behind him, and the
great general who had held plenipotential authority for
a number of years in a great war, and had perhaps
settled the affairs of half a dozen provinces, could hardly
be expected to return to Rome prepared to become
a nobody or to offer himself, once he had laid down
his authority, unarmed to the attacks of his political
enemies. Such was the trouble which confronted
Pompey when he returned from the East in 61 B.C., and
Julius Caesar when the time came for him to lay down
his command in Gaul in 49. The clash of these great
personalities and their parties was the discord out of
which the final harmony was achieved. Rome might
have external success. She could not have inner peace
until the legions were in control of a single man. Once
established, such a man might set Rome straight and
make the Empire a whole. It might have been, and

very nearly was, Julius Caesar. It turned out to be Caesar's heir, Augustus. Augustus (within whose reign Jesus Christ was born in Judaea) after a grim struggle gathered all the reins of power into his hands and put Rome's house in order. Under him, and not before, Rome's work in the world could begin.

Such, in outline, is the story of Rome's beginning. Crude as it is, it must suffice. For it is the aim of this book, not to delineate Roman history, but to describe what sort of a man the Roman was, what sort of a state he made himself, what sort of life he lived, and to explain in some measure why we consider him so important today.

CHAPTER II

THE ROMAN

Moribus antiquis stat res Romana virisque.—ENNIUS.

"On the old breed, the old ways, the Roman state stands strong."

WHAT sort of man was the Roman that he was able to do all this? The Romans of the great age of Rome were fond of asking this question. They liked to look back at what they conceived the development of the Roman character to have been, and this is the sort of answer they gave.

To begin with, the question would be better cast in the plural. For the most important thing about the Roman was his consciousness of the group to which he belonged. We first meet him as a member of a family, whereas the Greek of historical times is an individual. The family is ruled by the father, who demands implicit obedience from all its members and exercises absolute power within it. The mother, too, has her place and, though no less than her sons and daughters she is subject to her husband's rule, exercises a strong moral influence over the whole. Unlike the Greek mother, she is still on the family " strength " even after her child-bearing function is fulfilled.

The family lives a hard and simple life. It is a primitive agricultural community. They work hard to win their living from the soil, and, as Virgil constantly reminded his countrymen, " the great Father himself did not wish the farmer's path to be an easy one." And, if between the ploughing of one strip and the next they had to take their swords and fight to keep enemies off their land, it was all in the day's work. Human enemies were as inevitable as lamb-snatching wolves or as the rust-like blight which killed the young corn. The god to whom they sang to keep safe their crops was the god who could give them victory in battle. And when wars came to last from sowing-time to harvest, even then they did not question or complain. They obeyed because each of them knew that he too was potentially a head of a family who might one day have to be obeyed. This strong corporate sense held them uniquely together. Like the beating-rods, symbols of the magistrate's powers of chastisement, that formed the *fasces*, individually they might be weak; bound together they were strong. For the essential Roman obedience and command were the complementary parts of his Romanhood, the back and front of an armour which both held him together and made him invincible.

Life was hard and life was incalculable, but man must take things as they come and he must be serious. The terms which the Roman used to characterize this essential outlook were *gravitas* and *simplicitas*. The words have an obvious significance, but there is more to them than " gravity " and " simplicity," and they will repay elaboration.

The man who is *gravis* is the man who has a strong sense of his position. He sees himself as a member of society which owes him certain privileges and to which he owes certain duties. This society, moreover, is no chance affair; it does not live merely in the moment but is the ordered outcome of the experience of his fathers and an inheritance which he must keep ordered to hand on to his descendants. Thus the Roman has not only a strong civic sense but an innate respect for tradition. The Way of his Fathers (*mos maiorum*) was Law. Out of this respect for tradition springs a respect for *form*. The Roman is by nature a formal creature, because for him Order is enshrined in Form. This *formalism* was in itself a power for good so long as it operated within the sphere of a simple community and a simple life. But when the Roman came into contact with creatures more sophisticated than himself, and the setting of his life became more complex, this formalism hardened into something more dangerous. Forms began to be regarded for themselves, and the spirit was forgotten. *Conservatism* is a parallel aspect of the same character. Deeply aware of the past, the Roman was intensely anxious to preserve all the good he found in it. He was so set against revolution that he tended to forget the need for evolution; so obsessed by tradition that he was slow to adapt it to the needs of the present. In the end the adaptation always came, because events compelled it; but this unwillingness to accept change even when it was inevitable made Rome's career, it seems in retrospect, harder than it need have been. Fortunately, Rome throve on adversity, learning from her mistakes and in her very slowness achieving strength.

With this conservatism went the Roman's *exclusiveness*. The citizen who is acutely conscious of his city as a whole must inevitably regard it as something separate from the world at large. He will instinctively look upon those outside as " outsiders " (the term carries its own significance) and he will look down on them.

All these qualities are summed up in the word *gravitas*. The Roman is a " heavy " man; not an agreeable person to meet for those outside his circle, and not as go-ahead as you might expect in the world of men; but he carries big guns and has consequence as well as weight.

Gravitas describes how the Roman appeared to the outside observer. The other word *simplicitas* describes how he goes about his work. By nature and upbringing he is simple, that is to say, single-minded. He sees one thing at a time and goes about it. Only a simpleton, we say, follows his own nose; but it is a faculty commonly denied to those of superior vision and one not easily to be despised. It makes action possible where superior wits embarrassed with the choice between conflicting possibilities are at a loss. The Roman has, in fact, what in more charitable moments we call dispassionate good sense. He is not overblest with imagination.

This unimaginative good sense has two corollaries. The Roman is terribly in earnest. The life of the imagination, which unrelated to ends in action may assume, as it ultimately did among the Greeks, the proportions of a disease, has no meaning for the Roman unless it is directed to a practical purpose. The one branch of poetry in which he is at home is the didactic; he finds sense and point in a poem when it tells one how to run a farm, and it is significant that the first Roman poet wrote not because there was something inside him which had to be expressed, not because the Muses compelled him, but because he wanted a new school text-book for his pupils. Indeed, the bulk of Latin literature is either text-book or propaganda.

This earnestness may be all to the good for a life of action, but it makes a man poor when he comes to sit still. His human contacts will lack delicacy, and so, too, will his entertainments.   Roman humour, then, it is not so surprising to find, is as crude as the Roman outlook is matter-of-fact.   There is a pleasant story told by the Greek historian Polybius of a Roman official who had to give a large entertainment and on the advice of a Greek friend included a contest of flute-players.   To the disgust of host and party, to use Dr. Glover's words, it turned out to be something like a Welsh eisteddfod. But the skilful Greek grasped the situation in a moment. He slipped outside, gave a few necessary orders, and the bodies of flute-players marched on each other and proceeded to belabour each other over the head with their flutes.   The evening was a great success.   Nor in the realm of drama is it surprising that the slapstick farces of Plautus got larger audiences than the Terentian comedy of manners.   It is little use offering *As You Like It* to an audience which can only appreciate knockabout pantomime.   In one of his prologues Terence complains that his audiences desert him when they hear that there is a tight-rope-walking performance next door.

Wit, artistic taste, emotional sensibility: these are things in which the Roman was scantily endowed.   His wit was the wit of the farmyard and the barrack-square, the bludgeon not the rapier.   He had a sense of the useful, which for the artist is no bad start; but it is not enough.   Beauty is not entirely a function of utility. He could build an amphitheatre where 50,000 spectators at a time could watch gladiatorial and wild-beast fights, or baths where 3,000 could bathe at once; he could construct aqueducts with precision over long stretches of difficult country; he could bridge deep gorges and wide rivers.   These were the everyday needs of a busy empire, the practical expression of the society in which he lived.

If his bridges were beautiful, that quality was incidental. Self-expression was a thing which never troubled him. Thus his conscious art, when he came to pursue it, was firmly attached to reality. His sculpture dealt with real people, individuals, and did not strive after perfection of form, the ideal. The one significant contribution which he made to the fine arts was the art of the portrait-bust. And in emotional life generally the Romans were poor. There was little sentiment lost, as we shall see, in his love-making or in his attitude to nature; the passionate love of a Catullus and the *Weltschmerz* of Virgil are the exceptions which point to the rule.

In a word, the Roman lacked the *humanitas* (the sure sense of human values and of the part played by man in the universe) which made the Greek civilization great. The Greek saw life steadily and saw it whole; the Roman saw it steadily, but his vision was strictly limited, and it did not occur to him to ask whether he saw life whole. He saw life in terms of action and action in terms of his own needs; he never attained by himself to consciousness of the world of thought and to the vision of the ideals by which all right action must be governed. It is true and fortunate for posterity that he was inspired by Greek idealism to much of his greatest work, but in himself he remained the realist of the Western world.

Such was the Roman as, looking back, we can see him. But other strains entered his make-up. Foremost among these was that which is commonly called the Italian, a fairly old strain, distinct from what we conceive the Roman strain to have been, coming to Rome from without, yet present long before the age in which Rome shows any signs of being cosmopolitan. The Italian has the exuberance which the disciplined dour Roman has not; he is bright where the Roman is sombre, passionate where the Roman is collected. But he has not got the Roman's industry or concentration, and, if the Italian supplied the spark, it needed these sterner qualities to shape the Latin language and literature into its mature strength.

It has been observed that the great majority of Roman poets are by extraction Italian (Horace, for instance, came from Apulia, Propertius from Umbria, Catullus and Virgil both from over the Po), and Dr. Garrod in the Introduction to his *Oxford Book of Latin Verse* has singled out two adjectives which express to perfection what Latin literature owes to its Italian strain. The Muses, says Horace, gave to Virgil *molle atque facetum*, "tenderness and fire." "The Romans had hard minds," writes Dr. Garrod, "and in the *Eclogues* of Virgil" (the little vignettes of shepherd dialogue), "they marvelled primarily at the revelation of temperament which Horace denotes by the word *molle*; . . . that deep and tender sensibility which is the least Roman thing in the world and, in its subtlest manifestations, is perhaps the peculiar possession of the Celt." This tenderness (those who wish to explore it can find it brilliantly anatomized in Wordsworth's Preface to the Lyrical Ballads), which in Virgil "quivers beneath the half-divined sympathy with the Sorrow of the World, is of the same temperament as that which in Catullus gives to the mental anguish of the individual a universal poignancy." And the word *facetum* Dr. Garrod explains as primarily denoting fire (*fax* is the Latin for "torch"). For us *facetious* has come to mean little more than "cheap wit"; strictly the word should connote wit only in so far as wit is a thing which is bright and leaps up

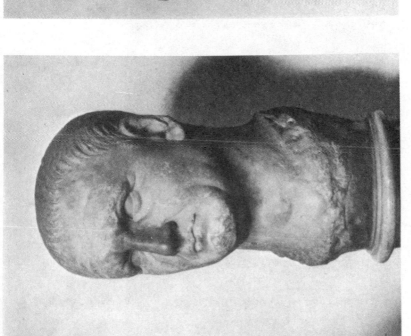

PLATE III.—ROMAN PORTRAIT BUSTS.

1. The Emperor Vespasian (A.D. 69–79): the hard-headed, efficient realist.

2. Vespasian's son, Titus (emperor 79–81): a more self-conscious, cultured type.

PLATE IV.—GRAVE-RELIEF OF L. AMPUDIUS PHILOMUSUS.

A family monument (father, mother, and daughter) belonging to the last century of the Republic.

suddenly in the mind as a flame from a black coal.
Together *molle* and *facetum* mean the fire of the mind,
the flame which is not merely quick and bright but the
index of a deeper and underlying heat by which it is
nourished.   It is the quick glow of sensibility.   In more
superficial verbiage it is the " brilliance " without which
literature is " dull."   On this side the Roman was dull;
the Italian was not.

The happiest text for the composite nature of the
Roman make-up is given, appropriately enough, by
Ennius, the father of Latin poetry.   He says in one of
his poems that he has *tria corda*, " three hearts," or, as
we should say, " three souls."   One is Oscan, that is,
native Italian; one is Greek; the other is Roman.
Ennius was Italian by birth, Greek by education, Roman
by adoption.   So it is throughout Latin poetry.   The
Italian strain provides the original impetus; Greek gives
the aesthetic element of form; Roman earnestness holds
the two together and sees the whole through.

I have spoken mainly in terms of poetry.   For in action
the Italian and Greek qualities in the compound hardly
obtrude themselves.   It is the Roman who conquers the
world.   During the process his character underwent
certain changes.   The Greek and other Mediterranean
influences with which he came into constant contact
during the course of world-conquest did that.   But the
old quality seems to survive late in the imperial age.
In the age of Augustus the *gravitas* and *simplicitas* are still
there.

Such was the official portrait.   In recent times
scholars exploring Roman origins have questioned its
authenticity.   They find the Roman a composite
creature from the beginning and suggest that the picture

3

of him as a stern and moral man of action was the invention of later centuries, a calculated piece of propaganda intended to bolster up the old order of things against the forces of revolution.   There is no doubt truth in the suggestion, but it does not invalidate the picture.   If the portrait is not a historical likeness, it gives us the standard which the Roman accepted as his own and which inspired much of the Roman achievement.   But on this point there will be more to say later.   The purists will find a similar discrepancy between the alleged characteristics of the Englishman and the genuine article; yet the Englishman of legend, of vulgar rumour and Continental renown, in the pages of history and of *Punch*, is no idle fiction; it is fiction calculated to illuminate intangible truth.

CHAPTER III

THE ROMAN STATE

Nostra . . . res publica non unius . . . ingenio sed multorum, nec una hominis vita sed aliquot constituta saeculis et aetatibus. . . .—CICERO.

" Our State was not the work of one mind or set up within a single lifetime. It was the outcome of many generations and many epochs."

ROME, as we have seen, was not built in a day. In the beginning, said the Romans, they had been ruled by kings, but no one knew where the kingly power had begun. In the year 509 B.C., they said, the kings, who were of foreign Etruscan stock, were expelled. And it is at that point that Roman history begins. There was no lack of legends about the foundation of the city or about certain of the kings; they were picturesque and here and there sensational. Through them we may descry a Rome materially flourishing under the domination of an alien dynasty, which was able to bring to it many of the arts and commodities of a maturer culture. But in popular sentiment and in the annals of history the period of the kings remained a Dark Age.

After the fall of the monarchy, the supreme office was shared between two officials (originally called " praetors," a title which was very soon changed into that of " consuls "). These were elected by the sovereign Assembly of the people of Rome, and held office for the duration of a single year. To them was delegated the *imperium*, the supreme executive authority in the affairs of state. Their power in practice was limited by

the provision that each could veto any action of the
other and that they must in important matters of state
consult the Senate, the body of elders and ex-magistrates,
all of aristocratic ranking, which was the survival of the
king's Council in the regal period.   Soon other magistrates were set up, to ease the burdens of the consuls:
the " praetors," to preside over the administration of
law; the " quaestors," to control finance; the " aediles,"
to superintend public works and the upkeep of roads and
markets.   In times of exceptional crisis, when decisive
action was imperative, the power of the consuls might
be suspended and given to a single leader, who was
called a " dictator." This was only an emergency
measure, and there was machinery to provide that when
the emergency was over the dictator resigned his power
and the consuls took over again.

The early age of the Republic was marked by the
struggle between the social orders into which Rome was
divided: the patricians and the plebeians.   The origin
of this split is obscure (it may have been the survival of
a distinction between an indigenous subjected population and a conquering race which settled in its midst),
but it is clear that it was in the main between a privileged
upper class and a lower class which was relatively un-
privileged and that the quarrel was both social and
economic.   In the early days only a patrician could
hold the office of consul, and no patrician could marry
a plebeian.   It took the plebeians two centuries to secure
political equality. This equality was, according to
tradition, largely achieved by a series of strikes on the
part of the plebeians.   They formed the majority of the
citizen-body and the bulk of the army in time of war.
If they were not granted their rights, they would not

fight for the State. By such means was won the first concession, by which it was enacted that certain officials should be set up within the magistrate body with the special province of protecting the rights of the plebeians; these were the tribunes of the plebs. That was in 494 B.C. In 471 B.C. it was enacted that these tribunes, as well as two plebeian aediles, should be elected by the plebeians organized in a new Assembly, the Assembly by tribes (regions into which the city was divided). Later the whole people came to be organized by tribes and this new Assembly became the recognized body by which new laws were passed. In the middle of the century the drawing up of the Twelve Tables, the first classic code of Roman law, was a further step in the process of reform; for up to this time law was unwritten, and the patricians exploited the general ignorance of law to gain their own ends at the expense of plebeians. Shortly afterwards marriage between the two orders was legalized, and soon came a law laying it down that any measure passed by the plebs in their plebeian Assembly should be binding on the entire citizen-body. In 367 B.C. was secured the right whereby one of the two consuls must be a plebeian, and in 172 B.C., when for the first time two plebeian consuls were returned at the same election, a chapter in Roman political history had been closed.

So the strife between patricians and plebeians was gradually eased, and to all appearance a complete democracy had been gained: the sovereign power was in the hands of the citizen Assembly, which passed all laws and elected magistrates. But a full democracy was never realized. Since Rome was continually at war, the consuls were as often as not away campaigning; further, their annual tenure of office made difficult any continuity of policy on their own part. But the Senate, which consisted mainly of ex-magistrates, was a permanent body of experienced statesmen. Thus it came that in the period of the great wars it was the Senate which in practice controlled policy and virtually exercised the supreme authority. It was the Senate that brought Rome triumphantly through the long ordeal of the Punic Wars, and men came to look on it as the backbone of government.

With the tension of the great wars over, with Rome well set on her career of Empire and open to new influences from abroad, the political atmosphere changed. The commercial classes multiplied and threw up a new aristocracy of big business and wealth (the " equites " or knights), whose demands frequently ran counter to the interests of the aristocracy of birth and public office. Participation in office was jealously guarded by a small select group of families. For once a man had held one of the higher magistracies he and his family automatically took rank as " noble." Until the last century of the Republic the aristocrats were remarkably successful on the whole in excluding the outsider from the Senate; but in the age of the great military leaders their grip, long maintained by political jobbery and imperial conservatism, steadily weakened until by the age of Caesar it was quite lost. By that time Rome was well set on the turbulent path which led to the cloaked monarchy of Augustus and his successors.

The Republican system had an elaborate scheme of magistracies, which the Principate of Augustus retained in outward form, though their powers were now subject to a higher control. Next to the consuls in importance came the praetors, originally two in number; as the tasks of Empire multiplied the number was from time to time increased until Julius raised it to sixteen; Augustus reduced it to ten, but the number stabilized itself under the Empire at twelve. Two of them were specially charged with the administration of justice; the others were governors of provinces. After the establishment of the standing courts (see page 56), they were presiding judges and in the year following their civil office provincial governors.

Every five years a pair of magistrates called censors, holding office for eighteen months, were elected. Their function was to keep the citizen roll, revising it, as well as the list of senators and equestrians, as they thought fit, and to exercise a general supervision over finance and public works. The censors were usually distinguished ex-consuls and, while in office, ranked in dignity, though not in power, over all other magistrates. During the last century of the Republic the censorship fell into abeyance and, though certain Emperors assumed its powers on occasion, played no part in the regular scheme of the imperial constitution.

Quaestors were assistants to the consuls in the financial administration of the State. Originally there were two; but the number was successively raised to four, then to eight, until under Sulla's system there were twenty, the majority of whom were financial assistants to provincial governors. Under the Empire twenty remained the regular number: two were urban quaestors, two were specially attached to the Emperor, two or four were assistants to the consuls, and the rest were provincial quaestors.

The aediles, whose function we have described, were

originally two in number and both had to be plebeians;
to these in time were added two more, called *curule*
aediles, of higher, patrician ranking, but it was not long
before the four posts were thrown open to plebeians.
To these Julius Caesar added two further plebeian
aediles Cereales, whose special province was the supervision of the corn supply. These six posts were retained
under the Principate, as were the ten posts of tribune of
the people, which were closely associated with them.

CAREERS

As early as 180 B.C. it had been laid down that magistracies should be held in a definite order, and minimum
ages for candidates had been fixed. Thus by the time
of Augustus it had become regular for the career of office
to follow a fixed course, graduating in successive levels
of importance till the consulate was reached. Augustus
added further stages and made the system rigid. By this
time, all real power being concentrated in the hands of
the Emperor, the republican magistracies became largely
sinecure appointments for the performance of routine
duties only, but they still went on; for the Emperor
sedulously kept up the republican façade, and the
prestige attaching to the ancient offices still attracted the
ambitious. Moreover, by passing through the regular
career of office, an able man might eventually secure
appointment to one of the really important provincial
posts in the imperial civil service.

The young man of senatorial birth began his career
by holding one of the group of minor magistracies known
as the vigintivirate and embracing various posts attached
to the courts of law, the police system and the mint.
After this he had to undergo a period of military service

for six or twelve months. When he reached the age of twenty-five he was eligible for the quaestorship, the lowest office to give entry to the Senate. The minimum age for the praetorship was thirty; between the quaestorship and the praetorship, the aedileship and the plebeian tribunate constituted an intermediate stage through which all plebeians had to pass; as almost all the offices in this stage were closed to patricians, patricians were excused this stage altogether. Two years' interval was statutory between the praetorship and the consulate, but for all but those specially favoured by the Emperor the interval was much longer. During this interval a number of important posts was open to the ex-praetor: posts on the staffs of provincial governors, commands of legions, governorships of certain lesser provinces and sometimes important treasury appointments. The minimum age for the consulate was thirty-three; originally there were two consuls each year; Augustus adopted the practice of having four consuls, successive pairs holding office for six months. In later reigns the practice of changing consuls every four or three or two months became common. The idea of this curtailment was to allow a greater number of deserving citizens to hold the supreme office and so to provide an additional supply of ex-consuls for use in the imperial civil service. Ex-consuls were eligible for the governorships of the senatorial provinces of Asia and Africa, or for the military governorships of such imperial provinces (see page 50) as Syria or Britain or for the coveted post of Prefect of the City.

We have copious records of such careers in the funeral inscriptions which survive many dignitaries of the imperial age. For the Romans lived by tradition, loved the external apparatus of power and were nothing if not monumental in their official life. Here is one such, the record of one Lucius Funinsulanus Vettonianus, which comes from a site in Croatia, once part of the Roman province of Pannonia Superior.

> *L. Funinsulano L. f. Aniensi Vettoniano, trib. mil. leg. VI Vict., quaestori provinciae Siciliae, trib. pleb., praet., legato leg. IIII Scythic., praef. aerari Saturni, curatori viae Aemiliae, cos., VIIvir. epulonum, leg. pro pr. provinc. Delmatiae, item provinc. Pannoniae, item Moesiae superioris, donato (ab imp. Domitiano Aug. Germanico) bello Dacico coronis IIII, murali vallari classica aurea, hastis puris IIII vexlis IIII, patrono d.d.*

We gather from the inscription that he was of the Aniensian tribe and bore the same first name as his father; that he began his career as a subaltern in the Sixth Legion Victrix (which at this time was quartered in Spain). He then went as quaestor to Sicily; came back to Rome to take office successively as tribune of the people and praetor; went out overseas to command the legion Fourth Scythica (which by this time was quartered in Syria); came back to civil office as Prefect of the senatorial treasury (a post open to ex-praetors), then as Commissioner for the great Aemilian Road (which ran from Ariminum to Placentia), and so at last attained the consulate and also secured a place in the select Board of Seven which supervised the observance of certain ancient religious ceremonials. After this he was successively governor of the important imperial provinces of Dalmatia, Pannonia and Upper Moesia, where he presumably died. The last two lines of the monumental inscription set up by a grateful dependant record Vettonianus's many military decorations.

It was also part of the set policy of the imperial settlement to provide a definite career of office for the class
of *equites*, such as it had never had under the Republic.
In the first stage of the equestrian career came periods
of military service, in which the young man was attached
as an officer to legions or auxiliary cohorts or engineering units or with duties at certain military depots; sometimes he went on to become a commandant in a section
of the City Guard (or Police), or of the Praetorian Guard.
Once these preliminary qualifications had been gained,
many administrative posts were open: financial inspec-
torships in imperial provinces; governorships of certain
small provinces administered by the Emperor; and the
six great prefectures which included commands of naval
stations, of the City Police, control of the corn supply,
and culminated in the powerful offices of Governor of
Egypt (which was always, because of its wealth, in a
category of its own) and of Prefect of the Praetorian
Guard. The great Secretaryships of State, too, once
occupied by personal freedmen of the Emperor, came to
be filled by *equites*. From the time of Hadrian Rome
had an elaborately organized civil service in various
well-defined grades filled exclusively from the equestrian
order.

Here is a typically equestrian career:

M. Petronio M. f. Quir. Honorato praef. coh. I Raetorum,
trib. mil. leg. I Minerviae p.f., praef. alae Aug. p.f. Thrac.,
proc. monetae, proc. XX hered., proc. prov. Belg. et duar.
Germaniar., proc. a ration. Aug., praef. annon., praef. Aegypti,
pontif. minori, negotiatores oleari ex Baetica patrono. . . .

Honoratus's career started with three military posts:
he was prefect of the First Cohort of Raetians, military

tribune in the First Legion Minervia (a legion of the Rhine-Danube front; the titles *pia fidelis*, " loyal and trusty," were conferred for loyalty in a time of mutiny and may be compared with such English regimental titles as " The King's Own ") and commander of a squadron of Thracian horse attached to the Eighth Legion Augusta (a legion of the Rhine front).   Then his career in the civil service began; he became a Mint official, then a commissioner for the collection of the (5 per cent.) death duty, then a revenue officer in Belgic Gaul and Germany, and after this experience became a man of mark, holding in turn the posts of chief financial secretary to the Emperor, of prefect of the corn supply and finally the Governorship of Egypt.

These records are typical of thousands of careers of imperial officials and indicate both the elaborate organization of imperial government and the value attached to experience.   To men of merit a wide field of public service was open and promotion assured in a system which had much of the stability of the British civil service of today.   One great difference between our British civil service and the Roman may be noted: the Roman was non-specialist: the same man might be called on to act as soldier, administrator, financial official, judge.   Whether such a system loses in efficiency more than it gains in solidity is a question not lightly to be answered.

ALLIES AND EMPIRE

So far in this chapter we have dealt with the domestic side of the Roman State, its inner workings of office within the citizen-body.   We must now turn to the outer aspect of the State, its relations with allies and dependants and the administration of empire. Just as the patricians within the Roman citizen-body had for long denied the plebeians a share in privilege, so for long the Romans as a whole denied citizenship to their allies.[1] Here as in many other phases of Roman development we find a curious mixture of assimilating impulses with conservative tradition. In the end they were compelled to extend privilege and to incorporate their allies within the State. But it was a slow process; even when this incorporation was an accepted policy various grades of privilege were rigidly maintained. It cost Rome a four-year civil war before she recognized the necessity of extending the citizenship to Italy, and it was not till the year A.D. 212 that full citizenship was extended to the Empire at large. Until that time the inhabitants of the Empire were variously classified; some had full citizenship derived from their Roman origin, some from their membership of a provincial community of honoured status, some had " Latin " or partial rights. Touring the provinces in the early imperial age, we should have found many towns far and wide in possession of the full rights: some because they had been from the start citizen-settlements sent out from Rome, some because they had received such " colonies " on top of an older foundation; some, old native communities because they had been expressly given the rank of Roman municipalities. Whether the town possessed

[1] The possession of Roman citizenship gave its holder three main advantages: it safeguarded his person from summary treatment by magistrates and other officials; it protected him in the various aspects of his private life (in his marriage status, his business activities, his holding and bequeathing of property) within the sphere of Roman law ; it gave him the right to share in the government of Rome by voting in the citizen-assembly and standing for public office.

complete or incomplete self-government, this did not materially affect the citizenship of its inhabitants. Contrasted with these we should have found towns with partial rights which were not incorporated in the Roman State but in theory lay outside it; their inhabitants were *peregrini*; most of them were bound to Rome by specific treaties in which their status was defined. Such were the *coloniae Latinae*, the *municipia Latina*, the *civitates liberae*, the *civitates foederatae*, the *civitates stipendiariae*; the shades of distinction between them are too complex to be set out here, but their maintenance illustrates the two guiding principles of Roman policy. The first was that newly-acquired territory should be bound to a definite status, the second that subject communities should be bound by *separate* treaties to Rome, to prevent their co-operation against her. Such was the purport of the wise maxim *Divide et impera*.

A province means strictly in Latin a " sphere of duty "; in the State it meant the group of duties assigned to a magistrate. As new territories came under the dominion of the Roman people they constituted new spheres of duty, and so the term *provincia* took on a geographical meaning. The earliest provinces were governed by praetors, and as more provinces were added the number of praetors had to be increased. As the number of annual magistrates in time was still too small to provide for the increasing needs of administration, a device was adopted whereby at the end of his year of office a magistrate might be retained in office for a further year. During this additional period he was termed an acting magistrate; he was said to be exercising authority not as the consul or praetor he might have been in the previous year, but *pro consule* or *pro praetore*. These

proconsuls and propraetors came to be regularly
employed as governors of provinces. At the end of
this second year a further renewal of authority was
possible. Thus it came about that provincial governors
(who were often great generals, as were Pompey and
Julius Caesar), after an extended period of office,
became so powerful that they outgrew the republican
scheme and made inevitable the institution of the
Principate.

Under the Republic provincial government was
largely the affair of the Senate, consisting as it did of
experienced ex-magistrates. The Senate supervised the
allocation of governors to provinces and had the dis-
cretion of extending a governor's tenure of office. During his term of office a governor had to send to the
Senate periodical reports, and any arrangements he might
make which were to hold good after his return had to
be ratified by the Senate; on his return to Rome he had
to render a full account of his governorship. Under
the Republic the provincial governor received no salary,
but was provided with funds to pay for food and other
maintenance expenses, for himself, his staff and his troops.
Any additional troops that the state of the province might
make necessary were brought from Italy and, military
office being scarcely distinguishable from civil, under
the direct command of the governor. The governor
took out with him a staff of lieutenants or *legati*, appointed by the Senate, though the governor usually had
a say in their choice. These could act as deputies for
the governor in both military and judicial capacities.
He had also a special financial officer in the quaestor
who went out with him, usually a young man just
beginning his public career. There were other assist-

ants, vaguely designated by the term *comites* (companions), often friends and relations of the governors.

With this suite and equipment the governor took over complete control of his province in the military and civil spheres alike, administering justice, keeping order and supervising the income of revenue. The costs of government were met by various forms of taxes. Where a direct land-tax or poll-tax was payable (*stipendium*), it was probably collected by the local municipal authorities and handed over to the governor's quaestor. The *decumae* or tithes on crops were collected by syndicates of tax-gatherers (the "publicans" of the New Testament), the farming rights being sold by auction to the highest bidder. The *scriptura*, a tax on cattle grazed on public land, and the various *portoria*, customs due on imports and exports, were similarly collected. Under the Republic the tendency was for Romans to regard the provinces as territory to be exploited rather than as lands for which Rome had assumed responsibility, and many a provincial governor, like Verres, made unscrupulous use of his period of office to fill his own pockets. Yet there was no lack of machinery for bringing bad governors to justice; from the year 149 B.C. there was a standing criminal court to deal with such offenders.

Though the imperial age brought many improvements into the system of provincial government, the republican system was not wholly bad. If it showed little sense of responsibility and little missionary urge in giving provincials a share in privilege or in imparting the Roman culture, on the other hand it allowed them to live their own lives. Rome imposed no rigid system of government, made few demands on the provincials of military

PLATE V.—IMPERIAL COIN PORTRAITS.

1. The Emperor Augustus (31 B.C.–A.D. 14).
2. The Emperor Claudius (A.D. 41–54).
3. The Emperor Trajan (A.D. 98–117).
4. Trajan's wife, Sabina.

PLATE VI.—IMPERIAL COIN PORTRAITS.

1. The Emperor Hadrian (A.D. 117–138).

2. The reverse, showing the figure of Britannia (the prototype of Britannia on our pennies), commemorates his activities in Britain. (S.C. = *Senatus Consulto*, " by decree of the Senate " indicates a bronze issue; the other coins figured in these plates are gold.)

3. The Emperor Antoninus Pius (A.D. 138–161).

4. The reverse shows the figure of Jupiter Stator, holding a thunderbolt.

service, and gave them peace within and protection from enemies without. The chief merits in the imperial system were that the central control over individual governors was strong where it had formerly been weak; that the financial administration was effectively re-organized; that provincials were given a voice and interest in the affairs of Empire. The Empire came to be considered as an organic whole; its frontiers were tightened and where necessary remoulded, the old distinction between Roman Italy and the provinces was broken down, and the work of civilization went forward as professed policy. To this end the cult of worship of the Emperor, as it spread evenly throughout the Empire, was a great help, holding up as it did an easily-accepted symbol of a common loyalty. To organize this worship there came to be in each province a body of local mag-nates called the *concilium*, which in time became the official mouthpiece of provincial opinion, with some of the powers of a representative assembly.

We have seen something of the working of the imperial provincial system in instances of imperial careers. Under the Empire the governor was far less the autocrat he had been in republican times; he could no longer inflict summary punishment on Roman citizens, for now there was the cherished right of the " appeal to Caesar," and Roman citizens were far more numerous; and his opportunities for self-enrichment were drastically cur-tailed by the existence of a financial officer, the *pro-curator*, who was not answerable to the governor but only to the Emperor himself. On the other hand, his livelihood and career were more assured; he had now a fixed salary, large enough to make the post worth while, and a certain prospect of further promotion if he did well. In his capacity as commander-in-chief of the army, the Emperor came to assume responsibility for provinces which particularly required the presence of troops, and the governors of such provinces, often the most important, were in theory his lieutenants, *legati Augusti*. Certain old provinces whose tranquillity was assured continued to receive their governors under the dispensation of the Senate in the old republican way. Appointments to the big military provinces were made by the Emperor, who usually took care to appoint a man well tried in the regular career of office; so too were the appointments to the small border provinces which, under the imperial scheme, were entrusted to men of equestrian rank. In this way, as in home affairs so in matters provincial, the Emperor had all the leading-strings of power in a strong centralized government. The result was the *pax Romana*, for which provinces and Rome alike could be grateful. The only sufferers were the old noble houses of Rome, the die-hards who had set their faces against the extension of privilege and against the coming of political reform and were slowly exterminated in the process by which Augustus came to the central power that made possible the solution of the old problems.

The Law

The Law was perhaps the most conspicuous legacy which Rome has left the world. Just as she drove roads through countries before unknown and made a well-charted organism of the Mediterranean world, so also she charted the complex of relations between man and man and between man and the State by a system which is the basis of our Western law. The process was similarly slow. The growth of Roman law is as gradual

as the growth of the Roman State and its history. Like
the State, it had so much to assimilate.

Most cultures can boast codes of law, lists of definite
rules to be obeyed; but such codes do not spring fully-
fledged into being. Behind a Hammurabi or a Solon,
behind the Hebrew Decalogue and the Roman Twelve
Tables stretches a long tract of time in which law is not
so much rule as custom. Men form habits in their
dealings with their gods and with their fellow-men, and
from these habits religious law, state-law, criminal and
civil law gradually evolve. Early in the civilized state,
indeed the civilized state is hardly possible without it,
man comes to look for guidance in these matters from
certain recognized authorities, kings, priests and small
bodies of priests. Before customs and rules are codified
and made clear for all to consult, the power of kings
and priests is supreme.

So it was at Rome. When the kingship was abolished,
the College of the king's advisers remained. For long
this small company of nobles had the sole authority in
matters of law; the lower classes were ignorant of the
law in the detail required for the conduct of religious
and social life, and the aristocrats were not slow to
exploit their monopoly in their own interests. When
the movement for reform came, one of the great cries
was for an open and published law (just as at the
Reformation one of the great cries of priest-ridden
societies was for an open Bible). It came. In the
middle of the fifth century B.C. the law was first codified
in the formulation known as the Twelve Tables. These
were variously indebted in inspiration to ideas borrowed
from other peoples in Italy and Greece, but in their
broadness, their hard terseness of expression, their

relative freedom from superstition, they were Roman. Much latitude for interpretation was, of course, still left; but law was once and for all out of the control of a class and open to all the citizens. Citizenship, of course, remained a highly exclusive right, and access to the law was the privilege which went with it. Then, as Rome's dominion spread through Italy, other peoples came within the law.

The administration of the law was in the hands of magistrates, the chief of whom was the *praetor*. This office had been expressly created for the purpose in the fourth century. Originally there was only one praetor; a second was appointed in the third century, the *praetor peregrinus*, whose duty it was to take cognizance of cases in which one or both of the parties were non-Roman; by the end of the Republic, as we have seen, there are sixteen praetors. In civil cases the praetor gave warrant for a suit to be brought, empanelled jurymen, made clear the point at issue and ordered execution of sentence upon the verdict given. On taking up his annual office the praetor published his edict, a notice setting out various points of interpretation and modification of the standing law which as praetor he proposed to follow during the year. In the main these edicts consisted of modifications of the law in the interests of equity. As edicts were published almost every year and carefully preserved, a great body of rules of equity gradually accumulated similar to the body of Case Law in our country.[1] This great mass, full of valuable precepts and contradictions, remained unsystematized till the reign of

---

[1] With this difference, that our Case Law is constructed from judgements from the judicial bench, whereas the Praetor's Edict consisted of what we should call counsel's opinions.

the Emperor Hadrian, when under expert lawyers the process of codification began.

There was no legal profession, as we know it, in ancient Rome. Praetors were not elected for their knowledge or skill in the law, and they held office only for a year. Nor was there any equivalent to our bar; anyone could plead in court, and in strict theory no fees for pleaders were allowed (though in practice there were ways round this embargo, even when it was regarded). Yet there were not lacking legal experts, men who made a study of the law, framed commentaries on difficult points and gave advice to those who needed it. The rulings of these learned authorities, too, went to swell the bulk of the materials from which Roman jurisprudence was made. These experts were not counsel but theoretic specialists, open for the consultation of pleaders, magistrates, litigants alike. During the third century B.C. a practice was introduced by which the jurist admitted an audience when he was about to give an opinion on a point. In this way a legal education became possible. Towards the end of the Republic a number of textbooks on law were published and the practice steadily continued, another contribution to the mass of material on the law.

Under the Empire Augustus went a step further. He gave to certain distinguished jurists the privilege of delivering opinions which were binding on judges and juries. The right (*ius respondendi*) was continued by the successors of Augustus and, as the *responsa* were given in written form and under seal, they came to constitute a separate body of authoritative literature possessing the force of law.

The work of systematizing this floating mass of literature, begun, as we have shown, by the codification of the Praetor's edicts in the time of Hadrian, was continued in the following reigns. Salvius Julianus, the official editor of the Edicts, compiled also a valuable Digest, an exposition of the working of civil law. Similar work was done by Papinian, who held the office of Prefect of the Praetorian Guard in the reign of Septimius Severus, when that office had become an entirely judicial one. Sextus Pomponius produced among other works a commentary of over eighty books on the now systematized edicts. Similarly prolific were the great authorities Paulus and Ulpian, both of whom in their time held office as Prefect of the Guard. Ulpian's *Rules*, a work for beginners, has survived, a cherished classic. But the greatest name is that of Gaius, a teacher and industrious writer, whose elementary manual, the *Institutiones* in four books, is more or less completely extant. It is an impressive work, written in forceful Latin without any of the pretentiousness from which legal text-books are prone to suffer, and remains a standard work for modern students of the law.

It is noteworthy that many of these great writers on the law were not Romans, but came from outlying parts of the Empire: Julianus came from Africa, for example, and Papinian and Ulpian from Syria. This is symptomatic of the process by which Roman law in its mature form came to be the expression not of a single nation but of a world. The slow broadening of outlook in law is characteristic of Roman development and can be seen in operation early in republican history. The inhabitants of the small city-state of Rome could not have intercourse with other peoples and tribes without discovering that there were other legal systems than their own.

Cases arose in which parties did not come under Roman law. What was to be done ? Roman practice came to consider Roman law and the alien law side by side, to extract what was common to both and to proceed on that. So gradually was evolved the conception of the " law of nations," *ius gentium*. At first this *ius gentium* was regarded as an inferior thing, at best a makeshift expedient for surmounting a practical problem. But as Rome's horizons extended and more peoples came within her bounds and philosophical inquiry deepened, a different estimate prevailed. Under the influence of Greek ideas, men began to see laws of nature and principles of humanity beneath the codes and conventions of different societies. Stoicism, which took a lasting hold on the Roman mind, preached the rights of man and helped to guide under the Empire the strong trend towards humanitarianism and broad equity which became increasingly marked in the first two centuries A.D., until it was caught up in the great Christian movement for which it had helped to prepare a way.

Roman criminal law grew slowly in the train of civil law. The idea of crime, offence against the State, is a later concept than that of civil wrong, offence against a fellow-man. Under the old order of Rome, the king had supreme power in punishing those who offended against the State; but sometimes he would delegate this authority to special officers and sometimes he would permit appeal after sentence to be made to the citizen-Assembly. When the Republic was set up, this appeal to the Assembly was made a basic right of all citizens, a right which was soon to be safeguarded by the institution of the Tribunes of the Plebs, whose particular province it was to protect a commoner against any undue exercise of power on the part of a magistrate.

Sentence under criminal law ranged from the death penalty by beheading or strangling, through various degrees of curtailment of citizen-rights, to the mere imposition of fines. Imprisonment, detainment at the State's pleasure, was not used by way of punishment. In republican times the death penalty was seldom inflicted and could usually be avoided by voluntary exile. By so doing the offender forfeited his citizen-rights and thereby put himself out of reach of the working of Roman law. As Rome grew and cases multiplied, appeal to the whole citizen-body became too unwieldy to be workable as a regular expedient. Instead the people set up by a legislative act a special Commission of Inquiry. In the first place, special Commissions were set up for particular cases, but during the last two centuries of the Republic standing Commissions for different types of offence came into being. In these was employed the jury-system, which already obtained in the hearing of civil suits. So there came to be special Courts for offences of extortion on the part of provincial governors (the *quaestio de rebus repetundis*); of embezzlement of public funds; of poisoning; of bribery at elections or trials; of promoting civil riot; of assassination; of forgery, coining and perjury; and, lastly, there was a Court for Treason, which could take cognizance of any act " by which the greatness of the Roman People was lessened " (a vague and elastic definition which could be perverted to serve unscrupulous ends, as it was under the early Emperors who used it to remove persons suspected of active opposition to the Emperor or his position).

These standing Courts were conducted by a magistrate, normally a praetor, who presided, heard the charge, empanelled a jury from the roll of those eligible to serve, received their verdict and passed sentence. Here there was no appeal to the People, since in theory the Court itself had been expressly set up by the People, but in some instances the case might be tried again by the same Court. There was no official prosecutor (any private citizen might take it upon himself to conduct the case as plaintiff), and the lack led to the bringing of malicious charges by irresponsible and unscrupulous persons, an abuse which got badly out of hand in several reigns of the early Empire.

Under the Empire there was a marked change. Though in outward form the old procedures largely remained, the motive power came from above, not from the citizen-body below. The figure of the Emperor came to dominate all, the sole head of the judicial system; now sitting as a judge in public courts, now delegating authority to his own nominees to act as judges, now constituting informal courts for the hearing of special cases. The Emperor's powers of intervention could give new vigour and direction to the old processes and could open up chances of appeal which under the old order had not existed. In this new scheme of things the Senate, deprived of its authority as the supreme advisory and administrative Council of State, came to function as a High Court of Law, in which the most serious political cases could be tried—*pour encourager les autres*. For here in the last resort it was the Emperor who had the say.

CHAPTER IV

FAMILY AND HOME

O quid solutis est beatius curis,
cum mens onus reponit ac peregrino
labore fessi venimus larem ad nostrum
desideratoque acquiescimus lecto.—CATULLUS.

" What happiness to shed anxieties, when the mind puts off its burden and worn with the labours of the world we come back to hearth and home and sink to rest on the pillow of our dreams! "

THE Roman word *familia* means more than our " family," and the Roman *paterfamilias*, the father of the family, had more responsibilities and more power than his modern counterpart. The *familia* included not only children but also the servants (who were slaves and were called *famuli*) and the *clientes*, the free dependants who looked to the *paterfamilias* as their patron or father-and-guardian. It also included the *manes*, the spirits of its dead forbears, and its *lares* and *penates*, its own private gods.

Thus the head of a Roman household was gravely aware of his position, standing between past and future. Behind him were the spirits of his fathers, whose ways had grown into present " law " and whose intent was now concentrated in his own person, to be diffused in turn into the lives of his descendants which lay before him. In the past he had himself been subject to his father's will; in the future his sons would become heads of families themselves; meanwhile he stood betwixt and between, the pivot of his race. Inside the family he was complete master; over his wife he held the authority of the hand (*manus*); over his children he held the authority of the father (*patria potestas*); over his slaves the authority of the master (*dominica potestas*). This authority was absolute and, if there were few fathers who, like Brutus, had the hardihood to put a son to death, legally the power was always there. Similarly, just as in the entire body politic *imperium* strictly belonged only to the sovereign people and was merely delegated to its successive holders, so inside the family property was held in theory only on the sufferance of the father. In the eyes of the State he alone held property.

MARRIAGE

Such was the organism which was the unit of the Roman commonwealth. Let us look at it a little more closely. We will begin with marriage; for, as Cicero tells us, marriage is the beginning of the State and the seed-bed of civic life. " For," he says, " since the desire to beget offspring is the natural property shared by all living things, the root of society is in marriage, its growth in the begetting of children, its consummation in the unity and community of the home." Marriage, then, was, for good or for bad, a matter of political wisdom; for good, in that it was the bond of the State; for bad, in that it might ignore to its own undoing the individual sentiment on which alone true marriages are founded. For good or bad, then, marriages for the Roman were a matter not of falling in love, but of prudence and arrangement. During the last two centuries B.C. marriages in the leading families came to be used increasingly to serve the ends of political pacts and alliances. To explore the frustrations and unhappinesses which such a practice must produce is no part of our present theme.   It is enough to say that if for Catullus passionate love was hell:

> *odi et amo. quare id faciam, fortasse requiris.*
> *nescio, sed fieri sentio et excrucior.*
>
> " I love and hate.   You ask how this may be.
> I only know its truth and agony."

for the typical Roman a dutiful marriage meant peace. The fire that consumed the heart of a Dido and overrode all sense of duty was a force against which the Roman conscience, in the shape of the good Aeneas, must fight to the death.

But we must not overstress this side of the picture. There is a joy which is not convention, yet so spontaneous that it could hardly be frowned on, in the marriage songs of Catullus:

Prodeas, nova nupta, si
Iam videtur, et audias
Nostra verba, vide ut faces
Aureas quatiunt comas:
Prodeas nova nupta.

Come forth, new bride!
So please you, come
And hear our song:
The torches shake their golden hair:
Come forth, new bride!

Tollite, o pueri, faces:
Flammeum video venire.
Ite, concinite in modum
" *Io Hymen Hymenaee io,*
Io Hymen Hymenaee."

Lift, lads, the torches:
I spy the veil.
And sing together as you go
Sing joy, sing wedding joy!

En tibi domus ut potens
Et beata viri tui,
Quae tibi sine serviat
(*Io Hymen Hymenaee io,*
Io Hymen Hymenaee),

See the rich house,
Your man's and yours,
Happy to wait in you its queen
(Sing joy, sing wedding joy!)

Usque dum tremulum movens
Cana tempus anilitas
Omnia omnibus adnuit,
Io Hymen Hymenaee io,
Io Hymen Hymenaee.

All yours till Age
That greys the hair
Shall nod assent
With trembling head to all for all:
Sing joy, sing wedding joy!

Transfer omine cum bono   Lift her little golden feet,
Limen aureolos pedes,   And, groom, good luck,
Rasilemque subi forem.   Over the threshold, past smooth door.
  Io Hymen Hymenaee io,   *Sing joy, sing wedding joy!*
  Io Hymen Hymenaee.

The colours of Catullus's songs may be emotionally heightened; but, whether it had its beginnings in romance or not, the love between Roman husband and wife could be a lasting, even imperishable, thing.

" Wife," writes another Roman poet in the last days of the Roman Empire, " let us live as we have lived; and let us cherish the names we first took on our wedding day; and I will always be to you the boy I was and you my girl, and let no day change us, as long as life shall last."

> *uxor, vivamus ut viximus, et teneamus*
> *nomina quae primo sumpsimus in thalamo ;*
> *nec ferat ulla dies ut commutemur in aevo,*
> *quin tibi sim iuvenis tuque puella mihi.*

Usque dum tremulum movens cana tempus anilitas omnia omnibus adnuit. . . . it is the same creed. Love is the armour against age.

WEDDING

There were various ways of marrying. The most elaborate ceremony was that exclusive to the aristocratic families called *confarreatio*, in which the couple ate together a sacred cake (*far*) which had been offered to Jupiter. This was a sacramental ceremony, and by it the bride was initiated into the religious life of her husband's family and became subject to his authority. In later republican times and under the Empire, with the growing freedom exercised by women, this form of mar-

riage became very rare, and forms were preferred in
which the bride, instead of passing completely into the
power of her husband, remained under her father's
authority and retained power to own and inherit in
her own name.

The simplest way was the arrangement by which if a
couple lived uninterruptedly together for a year they
might consider themselves married (an arrangement as
informal as the commonest form of divorce, by which
it was enough for the husband to send a letter to his
wife stating that he no longer wished to live with her).
In this form of marriage a wife could, moreover, remain
under her father's authority, if she wished, merely by
absenting herself from her husband for three days in
each year.

The plebeians had a marriage ceremony (*coemptio*), in
which the symbolism was that of a sale. In this the
bride's father or guardian went through a pretence of
selling her, in the presence of five witnesses and of a
person who held a pair of scales (a survival of the time
when money had to be weighed out) into the husband's
" hand."

Before the marriage a betrothal ceremony might take
place, at which gifts were given to the bride (gifts, which
could not, as with us, be recovered if the engagement
were broken). Among these was a ring, commonly of
iron, worn on the third finger of the left hand, from
which, it was believed, a nerve ran straight to the
heart.

By law a boy could marry at fourteen and a girl at
twelve; but it was not usual for a young man to be
married before the early twenties. The girl would usually
be between the ages of fourteen and eighteen. For

in the warm Mediterranean countries girls come to maturity much earlier in life than in the north.

On the eve of her wedding day the bride-to-be dedicated to the Lares of her home her toys and the bordered gown she had worn as a child. Her wedding dress consisted of a white tunic-dress woven straight down after the ancient fashion (the garment of the Gospel, "without seam, woven from the top throughout ") and tied round the waist with a woollen girdle in a "magic" knot, which only her husband might untie, and shoes of saffron yellow. Her hair, if all the old customs were to be observed, had to be arranged in a special way, in six tresses, which were divided by the points of a spear-shaped comb which was supposed to symbolize the time when men had captured their brides at the point of the spear. On her hair thus arranged she wore a garland of flowers which she herself had gathered and, over this, a large flame-coloured veil.

Early on the wedding morning the omens were taken, and the bridegroom came to the bride's home in toga and garland, accompanied by his relatives and friends. Once the omens had been pronounced favourable the bride and groom went into the atrium and before ten witnesses and the wedding company ceremonially clasped right hands. For this their hands were joined by the *pronuba*, a matron friend of the bride. And there the ancient formula was spoken, the equivalent of our " . . . in sickness and in health . . . till death us do part "—*Quando tu Gaius, ego Gaia* (" So long as you are Gaius, I am your Gaia," " Where you are Jack, I am Jill "). Then followed prayers and sacrifice (to Jupiter and Juno, especially, for she was the patroness of married life, and to the old gods of the fruitful field who would bless the marriage with increase), and, after that, the congratulations and wishes for good luck would come from the wedding-guests.   Then came the wedding feast, and, in the evening, when the evening star was rising, to crown all, the procession to escort the bride to her new home.

" Evening is here; rise up, my friends; the evening-star over Olympus
   Is lifting at last, at last his lamp long-waited;
   Time now to rise; time now to leave the rich-spread tables;
   Soon shall the bride come forth; soon the marriage-song be sung."

Such are the words with which Catullus begins one of his wedding hymns.   At the head of the procession went torchbearers and fluteplayers; the bride was attended by three boys whose father and mother must still be living (luck and superstition here played an important part), one carrying a torch of white-thorn in front, the other two walking one on each side of her.   She carried three coins, one to be offered to the gods of the cross-roads, one to the gods of the new home and a third, in token of her dowry, she kept for her husband.   Behind her walked an attendant bearing the distaff and spindle, symbols of home-life, and, last of all, came the wedding party, crying out the old invocations to the Marriage-God *Hymen*, singing old, ribald songs, and the boys scrambling for the nuts which the bridegroom scattered about him as he went along (the ancestor of our rice and confetti).

When they reached the house the bride anointed the doorposts with oil and fat and wound them with wool in token of dedication to a god.   In case she should stumble and so bring bad omen, she was lifted over the threshold, after which she repeated the simple formula

PLATE VII.—SCENE IN A ROMAN SCHOOL.

The master sits between two pupils, who hold books, and scolds a third who comes late.

PLATE VIII.—POMPEII, HOUSE OF THE SILVER NUPTIALS.
The atrium with peristyle beyond.

of devotion, *ubi tu Gaius ego Gaia*, and was met in the
Hall by the bridegroom who presented her with the
fire and water which were the symbols of house and
home. With the torch the bride lit the fire on the
hearth, then threw it to the guests to be secured by some
quick hand as a lucky keepsake. Lastly, after a prayer
for married happiness, the bride was led by the pronuba
to the marriage-couch set waiting in the Hall, and the
guests departed and left husband and wife together.
Such was the order of a wedding in the old style of
Roman life.

Roman history and legend is rich in stories of noble
women and devoted wives. Lucretia, Cornelia the
mother of the Gracchi, Porcia the wife of Brutus, Octavia
the sister of Octavian who married the triumvir Antony,
Arria the wife of Paetus Thrasea are an epic in themselves. Touching memorials can be found to them,
long and short, among the funeral inscriptions that have
come down to us. How eloquent is the four-word
epitaph of a certain Roman lady: *domum servavit, lanam
fecit*. That is all: " she kept her home, she span her
wool." And here is a longer, the testimony of a
bereaved husband of the time of the civil wars at the
end of the Republic to his dead wife Turia:

" You were a faithful wife to me and an obedient.
You were kind and sweet and responsive. You
worked devotedly at your spinning. You kept the
religious rites of your family and state and admitted
no foreign cults or low magic. You dressed quietly
and did not seek to make display in your household
arrangements. · Your attitude to our whole household
was a shining example; you tended my mother as
lovingly as if she had been your own. . . ."

5

Unfortunately, the marriage was childless, and the sorrowing husband goes on to tell how Turia, in all love and anxiety, suggested that he should divorce her and marry another wife who might give him children.

" You meant to secure a worthy life for me. You relied on the harmony of our souls. You assured me that the children to come should be ours and loved by you as your own. . . . I was beside myself with dismay. I could hardly pull myself from the horror I felt at your plan. That we should think of separating otherwise than by death! That you could imagine any reason for ceasing to be my wife while life endured, you who had been so true to me who had been almost an outlaw! What yearning, what need for children could I feel so great as to cause me to abandon honour, throwing away certain treasure for a speculation ? Enough. You stayed with me. . . . Now all content I had in life is lost with you. When I think of you, my ever-watchful protector in the hour of danger, I am crushed beneath the burden of my calamity and forget my vow. . . . I pray that your blessed shade grant you quiet sleep and keep sure watch over you."

CHILDREN

When a child was born it was in the power of the father to decide whether he would acknowledge it and bring it up. He would acknowledge it by lifting it from the hearth at his feet. On the ninth day there would be a ceremony of purification, and the child would receive the name, the *praenomen*, corresponding to our Christian name; *Publius* it might be or *Marcus* or *Sextus* or *Gaius*. And there would be little presents for the child, a string of little tinkling shapes called *crepundia* (" tinklers ") and a locket (of gold, it might be, for a rich man's son; of leather for the child of humble parents) called a *bulla* and containing an amulet; all intended to be charms against the power of the evil eye. A boy would wear the *bulla* until the day when he put off the garb of childhood and became a Roman citizen, the girl until the eve of her marriage.

With the Romans the home was a strong and lasting force, the bedrock of society. Mothers and fathers took pride in giving their children their first instruction, we are told. Here is the picture presented by Tacitus, writing in a more complex age of the old days:

" In the old days every Roman child born in wedlock was brought up at his mother's knee and under her sheltering hand, not in the back-bedroom of some slave-girl nurse. The mother took pride in keeping house and in giving herself up to her children, and looked for no higher praise. Moreover it was their wont to seek out some relative, some lady of matron's age and of approved worth, to whose guidance they could safely entrust the children of the house. In her presence shameful words and all actions which might seem mean or dishonourable were forbidden. And she guided not only their studies and exercises but their play too, where her wholesome modesty was an ever-refining influence. So it is that we read how Cornelia the mother of the Gracchi and Aurelia the mother of Caesar and Atia the mother of Augustus ruled over the early upbringing of their sons and brought them up to be leaders of men."

And here is the way in which Cato brought up his sons:

" As soon as the boy showed signs of intelligence, his father took charge of him and though he had an accomplished slave who was a schoolmaster . . . himself taught him to read. Cato was of the mind that it was not right that his son should be scolded and have his ears pinched by a slave when he was slow at his lessons, still less that he should owe to a slave so priceless a thing as education. True to this conviction he took it upon himself to be the boy's reading-master, tutor in law, and physical trainer. He taught his son not only to throw the javelin and to fight in arms and to ride, but also to box, to endure heat and cold and to swim strongly in the currents and rough water of the Tiber. We have it on his own witness that he wrote out in a large hand his own History of Rome, that his son might have in his own home a guide to the knowledge of the ancient traditions of his country. . . ."

EDUCATION

When the time for schooling came, there were first, as with us, the elements of reading, writing and arithmetic to be learnt. In a rich household the children might learn these elementary processes from one of their father's slaves. Many a father indeed might go out of his way to acquire a well-educated Greek slave for this purpose. But most boys would go for their first formal schooling to the school (*ludus*) kept by the *litterator* (" the teacher of letters "). Here they would use the wax tablet, the pointed stilus of bone or ivory (such as can be seen in abundance in many a museum in any land where the Romans ever lived); for tablet and stilus were the notebook and pencil of the ancient world. Later on they would learn to use ink and paper. For learning numbers there was the help of the *abacus*, or counting board, beads strung in frames such as one sees in nurseries today. While he was of preparatory school age he would learn by heart the Twelve Tables of Roman Law and strings of ancient moral precepts couched in ancient form.

School hours were early. The satiric poet Juvenal remarks that the wretched schoolmaster has to begin his work at an hour when no artisan or wool-carder is astir, and that the school-copies of Horace and Virgil get grimy from the lamps which the boys bring to school to work by in the early morning. And Martial in mock indignation curses the usher who is at it " with his truculent drone punctuated with beatings," breaking the slumbers of peaceful folk, before the cocks begin to crow.

Nor were there long vacations as with us. There might be many single holidays on festival days when all Rome kept holiday; but work went on through the hot summer months. It is interesting to find Martial pleading for a long vacation: " Mr. Schoolmaster, have a heart for your young innocents," he writes in one of his epigrams. " The July days are scorching hot; the light is glaring; the harvest-fields are parched and roasted. A truce to your birch and rod of office. Let the dear children sleep till mid-October. Good health is all the education they want in summer."

As for beatings, they seem to have been as plentiful as they were in the schools of Victorian England; Horace's *plagosus Orbilius* (" the man of blows ") has become proverbial, and the thoughtful Quintilian, the one great writer on education that Rome produced, is at pains to deprecate a practice which must have been widely prevalent.

At the age of twelve or thirteen the boy would go on to study under the *grammaticus*, to begin what we should call his secondary education. It is significant that, where the Roman elementary schoolmaster is called by a Latin name (*litterator*), the teacher in the higher stage has a Greek label (*grammaticus* is simply *litterator* in Greek). In the third century Rome began to come into continuous contact with Greek civilization, and the *grammaticus*'s school is one of the many instances of the desire to profit from things Greek. Greece to the Roman as he began to be aware of things beyond his own horizon meant new worlds of knowledge, and in these new schools, modelled on Greek schools, Rome set to work to learn its lore.

With the *grammaticus* the boy would learn grammar, history, geography, mythology (the study of the legendary past in things human and divine, the family tables of the gods, the stories of the ancient kings of Rome, enriched by an ever-growing consciousness of the illimitable depth of Greek literary lore receding into a dim past). These subjects he would pursue not systematically, as these and kindred subjects are pursued in the schools of today, but in parenthesis and digression as points of interest emerged from the study of literature. Not that such a procedure was as doubtful and precarious in results as it might at first seem. The study of great literature, above all of the *Iliad* and the *Odyssey*, and later of Virgil and Horace, is rich in the humanities and under the guidance of an intelligent master might inspire a lifelong interest in the map of knowledge and the world of men, such as has been gained by many a public-school boy at the feet of a rambling and unmethodical form-master. We can only surmise that the quality of the result must then, as now, have depended largely on the teacher; Dr. Dryasdust could nail down the letter and kill the spirit as surely as a well-equipped and sympathetic master could kindle and inspire.

The books that the Romans used were in the form of

rolls. In ancient times the bark of trees had been used for writing on and the memory survives, long after the practice had been abandoned, in the Latin word for " book," which is *liber*, and means " rind " or " bark." But in the times which we have in mind " paper " was made from the Egyptian *papyrus* plant (hence the name): a pleasing yellow-brown paper, light and thin and easy on the eyes of the reader in the glaring Southern light, but expensive and very liable to tear and crack. Parchment, made of animal-skins, came also to be used, but for its bulk and heaviness was considered inferior. We must imagine text-books, then, as rolls of papyrus. The text was arranged (all written out by hand, of course, for there was no printing in the ancient world) in columns extending from the top to the bottom of the roll's width. The reader held the roll in both hands, unrolling with his right hand as he read on and rolling up with his left the part he had read. Hence the word " volume," which means something rolled (*volvere*). Books were stored endwise in shelves, which might be pigeon-holed, and were carried about in round boxes.

From the school of the *grammaticus*, well-versed no doubt in the writings of Homer, of Plautus and Terence, perhaps of Virgil and Horace and Livy, and well-practised in the written and spoken word, at the age of sixteen or thereabouts the boy would go on to complete his formal education under the tuition of the *rhetor*, the teacher of rhetoric. This transition would usually come about the time at which the boy put off the purple-bordered toga of childhood and assumed the plain white toga of the man. So it is with us; we are " boys " at school, even though we are prefects and praepostors, but undergraduates have put away childish things and are

" men." The young Roman's university course, if such
we can call his period with the *rhetor*, was directed almost
solely to a study of the arts of speaking. At this stage
the pupils would be fewer and more select. Most of
them would be those who were marked for a public or
political career. For in ancient times the art of speaking
had an importance which cannot be gauged from a
consideration of its value in the modern world. We
have newspapers, a constant flow of print in book,
pamphlet and leaflet form, and broadcasting. In a
world in which print and broadcasting were non-existent
and publication negligible it was the public speaker who
swayed policy and dominated public opinion. Accordingly, to estimate the insistence on rhetoric in Rome,
we must add together in our minds all that journalism,
publishing, advertisement and radio mean for modern
times, subtract a little that goes for disinterested entertainment, and weigh the rest against the single word
" rhetoric." It is because we have come to rely less on
the spoken word and therefore to appreciate less the skill
shown in its use that the word " rhetoric " has come to
connote the high-flown and the ornate. We have come
to regard as a luxury what for the ancient world was
a social necessity, the art of effective expression.

In the rhetoric school the young man's time would be
spent composing speeches on all sorts of subjects and
themes and practising delivery. Since so many different
exercises would be required, it is only to be expected
that some of the themes were far-fetched. Unlikely cases
and situations would be invented to train the budding
barrister's ingenuity in debate; well-worn historical
themes would be argued over and over again. Whether
Hannibal after the battle of Cannae should have

marched straight on Rome must have been debated more often than the justification of Charles I's execution has been in the debating societies of English schools. Another King Charles's head was the retirement of Sulla: consider Sulla's position after he has seized supreme power and reformed the Roman State; should he retain his power or retire to a comfortable private life?

There was no vocational training of an organized educational kind except for those who were to be, in one capacity or another, public speakers. The more technical callings came more and more to be left to foreigners. And education generally remained a matter of private arrangement. Though occasionally rich men might on their own initiative endow schools in certain places, as Pliny did at Comum, and though under the early Empire certain provision was made to enable poor children in various districts to go to what schools there were, Rome had no state-appointed or state-controlled schools. And, though sometimes salaries were officially granted to deserving teachers, to the end she did not officially require education of any of her citizens.

So far we have spoken of boys, but have said nothing of the education of girls. It seems that girls might go to the same elementary schools as their brothers, for we find the poet Martial calling a certain schoolmaster " hated of boys and girls alike." But for the most part girls were brought up at home, learning the elements of housewifery from their mothers. This did not necessarily debar them from the culture which comes from a more formal education. In an enlightened household girls might well share the intellectual life of the menfolk, might even in a rich family have tutors of their own.

Cornelia, for instance (the mother of those two heroic reformers Tiberius and Gaius Gracchus), and Servilia (the mother of the Brutus who helped to assassinate Julius Caesar) were well-versed in the common currency of circles which turned to Greek philosophy as the well-spring of its intellectual life; and at a later date the satirist Juvenal has occasion to lament among other feminine types which meet with his disapproval the blue-stocking and the highbrow. Cicero, on the other hand, in an earlier age has occasion to praise women as the stronghold of the older culture against the invading forces of cosmopolitanism in public life. "Women," says the orator Crassus, speaking in a Ciceronian dialogue, "find it easier to keep the old ideals un-tarnished; they don't have so many people to talk to and they hold on all the more to their childhood lessons. When I hear my old grandmother speaking, it's like listening to one of the old classics, to a Plautus or a Naevius."

At the age of sixteen or seventeen, as we have said, about the time that he would be leaving the hands of the *grammaticus*, the upper-class Roman boy would put off the gold amulet-case and the purple-edged toga of childhood and put on the plain white garb of manhood. He was now ready for full citizenship. By this time the sons of lower-class parents would be hard at work in their various trades and callings. The rich man's son might supplement his time with the *rhetor* by a year or so of study at a Greek university or at Rhodes (whither Julius Caesar was going for this purpose at the time of his adventure with the pirates). Or he might go at once into the army to serve on the staff of some general a first apprenticeship in the arts of war. Or (and

instances of this are rarer) he might attach himself, as
Cicero did, to some lawyer or politician, with him to
absorb experience of public life in Rome.

The physical side of education was a matter for
private initiative. There were for those whose fathers
cared to arrange for the appropriate and necessary
patronage the time-honoured exercises in the Campus
Martius, riding, running, wrestling, boxing, jumping
and throwing the javelin. Fathers of the old school
would, like Cato, personally supervise their sons'
physical exercise and training. And most young
Romans would learn to swim in the exacting currents
and temperatures of the Tiber. There were certain
games of the organized, competitive kind which are the
mainstay of physical education in our schools (there
were one or two games of handball, for instance, varying
in the size and make-up of the ball and the number of
the players), but they seem to have been games for odd
moments, like billiards or club squash rackets, and we
hear comparatively little of them.

SLAVES

After the children of the household came the slaves.
In early times, when Rome was mainly an agricultural
community of small farmers, slaves must have been
comparatively few. Slaves were originally prisoners of
war. When Veii was captured by the Romans in the
fourth century B.C., its free population, Livy tells us,
was put up to auction. Also in times of economic de-
pression debtors might become slaves. But it was only
in the age of the great wars that the numbers of slaves
appreciably increased. Great wars meant many prisoners, and many prisoners meant cheap slaves, and the

demand rose with the supply. Great slave-markets were established, as at Delos, the tiny but central island in the Aegean, where at its height, according to the geographer Strabo, tens of thousands of slaves might change owners in a single day. Asia Minor became a great slave-hunting ground and the growth of the demand for slaves set a new premium on the kidnapping industry, which by the beginning of the first century b.c. had become a racket of such proportions that it needed a Roman navy and a succession of admirals to suppress it. In his Notebooks on the Gallic War Caesar casually mentions that the proceeds of a single Gallic town which he had occasion to destroy amounted to 53,000 slaves. Even the elder Cato in his time could regard the slave-trade as a profitable speculative industry and was not above buying up slave-children like so much live-stock to sell at a profit when they grew up. Prices naturally varied according to quality. The normal price for an ordinary unskilled able-bodied male slave seems to have been between £15 and £20. A skilled slave, a clerk or a doctor, might fetch £50 or more.

A fairly sharp distinction may be drawn between the slaves of the town house and those of the country estate. In the *familia rustica* slaves were frequently treated purely and simply as cattle, especially on the large ranches. On a small farm (Cato recommends for a farm of 240 *iugera* a staff of eleven labourers with a slave-bailiff and his wife to manage and look after them) they might be treated more or less as humans. But personal contacts were impossible between masters and the thousands of slave-labourers who worked on the big farm-estates which became common in Italy in the last two centuries

B.C. There conditions were inhuman; frequently slaves were driven hard all day and chained together in underground barracks at night. Where, as on the big cattle-ranches, slaves could not be strictly supervised, it is not surprising that slave-revolts were frequent and alarming. But by imperial times the abuse had largely died away. Wars were rarer, slaves harder to come by and dearer and, accordingly, better treated. In the town house, however large the establishment might be, a slave had a better chance of winning his master's respect, perhaps even his freedom. It is difficult to generalize about numbers; but there is evidence to indicate that an ordinary upper-class Roman of the time of Cicero who could show only ten slaves was barely respectable, while a retinue of 200 might be considered bad form in the other extreme. In the early imperial age a man whose hall-porter had other jobs to do or who could not afford an expert carver to serve his dining-room, and attractive young slaves to wait at table, was socially not worth knowing.

The normal upper-class Roman would have in his household (such a household as would in these days in England be served by three or four maids in regular employ and no more) a valet, if not a barber and a private physician as well, cooks, waiters, pastrymakers, kitchenboys and footmen, litter-bearers, a butler, a doorkeeper, housemen to keep the rooms clean, a steward and a secretary, all slaves and many of them well-educated men. Some of them would be trusty slaves inherited from his father, some of them might be legacies or presents from his friends or picked up by himself in the slave-market. Some of them might have been born and bred in the house. Some of them, especially perhaps a nurse or a tutor, might be old friends of the family; some of them might barely be known by name. Here perhaps were eight stalwart Cappadocians or Bithynians (Catullus has an amusing little poem on the chance of a staff-officer's picking up such a set cheap out East), bought specially to bear my lady's litter. Here perhaps a Greek of good birth and upbringing, kidnapped in his early 'teens from some town on the southern coast of Asia Minor, who could write a good hand and had a head for figures and made an excellent accountant's clerk; here a curly-headed page-boy from Spain, who got so many tips from visitors that he was saving up in the hope that one day his master would let him buy his freedom. Of course, his master might simply commandeer the lot and do nothing about it, and he would be perfectly within his rights. On the other hand, he might be kind and give him his freedom. In the formal ceremony of setting a slave free (called " manumission," i.e. a sending forth from the hand of the master) master and slave appeared before a magistrate; the slave put on the conical felt hat, which was, according to ancient usage, the freeman's badge, and knelt at the magistrate's feet. An attendant touched him with a rod, and the master lightly struck him with his hand as a symbol of the power he was giving up (the ceremony may be compared with the traditional ritual whereby the King confers knighthood), and the slave was declared free. There were other simpler ways of giving a slave his freedom; the master might do it by word of mouth in the presence of witnesses or by a letter or in his will.

Since the freed slave or freedman, as he was now called, frequently maintained close contact with the household in which he had served, and to which he might owe certain debts of gratitude, we may pause for a moment to consider his position. He was now a Roman citizen and, though some stigma necessarily attached to himself, there was no reason why his son should not lift up his head among the citizens at large. The poet Horace never sought to conceal the fact that he was the son of a freedman and even took a degree of pride in the fact; his father had been a good father and had given his son his chance in the world, and the son had nobly availed himself of it. On manumission the freedman put from him the single name by which he had been known as a slave (his barbarian name, it might be, or perhaps the name of his race—Syrus, Thessalus—as a workman today might be known to his familiar mates by no other name than Paddy or Sandy or Jock). Now he had a right to the free man's three names (he became, in popular phrase, a " three-name " man) and usually took his master's first and middle names. For, though he was now his own master, he would normally feel a close obligation to his old master and indeed be largely dependent, in many instances, on his support. During the Empire many freedmen rose to great wealth and influence. A great man might find his best confidants and an Emperor his safest and surest secretaries among his freedmen; and sometimes a freedman behind the scenes might wield power which it would have been dangerous to entrust to men higher in the social scale. The position of Claudius's freedmen, for instance, was in effect that of Cabinet ministers or Secretaries of State. And in Italy and the provinces freedmen were given the special privilege of organizing the local worship of the Imperial house which became a bond of Empire.

CLIENTS

The *familia* also included the clients (*cliens* meant originally " one who gives ear," i.e. to others).   These were dependants, poorer persons who were attached to the family and looked to it for protection and help of all kinds.   In the early days of Rome only patricians were citizens and all others, including in great measure new settlers and defeated enemies, had no legal standing in the Roman commonwealth and had to put themselves under the protection of citizens.   In return for the patronage afforded by the patron, the client paid his patron a regular and deferential respect.   He might work in his fields and, in a later age when men of consequence were no longer farmers but urban gentlemen, he would attend at his patron's house every morning and accompany him when desired as he went about his public occasions.   Such a relationship would be handed from father to son.   In theory this was an admirable arrangement and brought good to both parties.   Later, when slaves were more important and clients were citizens, the institution degenerated.   Clients tended to become parasites, expecting little from their patron but a money or food dole and giving nothing in return but a servile flattery.   We know them in the pages of the satirists as crowds of good-for-nothing hangers-on, jostling each other at the doors of the rich for precedence in the dole and noisily supporting their patrons as they went their ways, a picturesque but unsavoury aspect of the unemployment problem in imperial Rome.

FUNERALS

After life, death; and when a man died the ceremonies that marked his passing were no less elaborate than

PLATE IX.—POMPEII.

1. Hall of a house, decorated with frescoes.

2. Shop, showing election posters (painted up in red).

PLATE X.—BUTCHER'S SHOP.

The customer, sitting on the left, gives her order. Note the butcher's block and cleaver and the accuracy with which the joints are delineated.

those of the other cardinal points of his life.   For death
was no mere personal adventure; while the dead man
went " on the darksome path to that place from which
they say no traveller returns," as Catullus sings, his
death was an event in the progress of a family.   In the
eyes of the living it was that which joined a man to the
company of his fathers, the *maiores*.   *Manes*, the Latin
for the spirits of the departed, has no singular.

As he died some near relative would kiss his lips to
catch his last breath, and when he was dead the assem-
bled company would cry out thrice upon his name, as
if to ensure that he was dead indeed.   The eyelids were
then closed, and the body was washed and anointed and
wrapped for the last time in the toga and then laid in
state on the funeral couch in the atrium with its feet
pointing to the door through which it would soon go never
to return.   Between his teeth might be placed a penny
to pay his fare to Charon, the ferryman of the dead,
when he should cross the river Styx, the first of the rivers
of Hell which, in the ancient myth, the soul of the dead
had to cross.   At the door of the house was set a branch
of cypress (the mourning tree which clusters to mark
with its stark trimness many a cemetery in Italy and
Greece to this day), of cypress or of pine, to warn the
outside world that the house was under the pollution of
death.

A poor man might be buried quickly with all possible
despatch; a great man might lie in state for days, and
his funeral would be a solemn public ceremony.   A crier
would go out and cry *Ollus Quiris leto datus; exsequias
quibus commodum ire iam tempus est.   Ollus ex aedibus
effertur* (" Such a one, a citizen, has been given to death.
For those whose pleasure it is it is now time to attend

6

the funeral. He is being carried forth from his house ").
When the time for the carrying forth came, the procession was marshalled and set out. Though it is daytime
there are torches. For once upon a time funerals took
place by nights and the torches remain, like the tall
candles in the sunlight of an Italian funeral today.
First the musicians with trumpet and pipe; then the
hired wailing women, crying and beating their breasts;
then the death-masks (*imagines*) of the family's ancestors
worn on the faces of men who walk to impersonate
them; then the dead man's trophies and the dead man
himself. He lies on a couch of purple and gold, his face
uncovered, open to the air, borne by freedmen or slaves.
Behind follow the family, his clients and friends, the men
in the dark toga of mourning, the women in white without colour or gold upon their dress. In the Forum the
procession might pause for a kinsman to deliver a
funeral eulogy of the dead man's life, as Antony did at
the burying of Caesar. This done, the procession re-
forms and moves on through the city-gate to the place
of burial beyond the walls. For no burial is allowed
within the city.

In the earliest days of Rome the dead were usually
buried, but archaeology attests the existence of crema-
tion side by side with burial in the first beginnings of
human settlement on the site of Rome, and in the historic period from the fifth century B.C. onwards crema-
tion came more and more into usage and soon became
the normal procedure, except for certain distinguished
conservative families, such as the Cornelii, and for the
poor, who found burial cheaper. But under the later
Empire the influence of Christianity brought a general
reversion to burial.

The funeral pyre was built of pine-logs piled and decked with cypress-branches to look like an altar. On this the dead man was laid, and, with him, the wreaths, the incense and the sundry offerings of the mourners. Amid the lamentations of the funeral company a near kinsman with averted face set fire to the pile. (Such a scene can be read to the life in Virgil's account of the funeral of Misenus in the sixth book of the *Aeneid*.) Quickly the pyre would blaze up, glow and burn down. Then the last embers were quenched with wine, the mourners called on the dead for the last time *Ave atque vale* ("Hail and farewell") and, after being sprinkled three times with water to release them from the pollution of death, went their ways. Only the near relatives must stay to collect the charred bones and the ashes of the dead. The bones are washed with water and with wine, the ashes are mixed with perfume. Together they are placed in an urn of marble or bronze. The urn is taken away to find a resting-place on a ledge in the family tomb, a tomb such as any one of the greater tombs which the traveller may still see as he goes along the Appian Way two or three miles out of Rome.

We may fitly conclude this section with glimpses of Roman thought about death caught in literature: two of human pathos, and one of philosophy. First, an epigram of Martial on a little slave-girl, as fragile as its subject:

"This little maid, my father and mother, I commit to your care in the dead world—her who was my darling and my joy, that the little Erotion shrink not in fright of the black shades and of the monstrous jaws of the Hound of Hell. She would have lived the full span of her sixth winter, had she lived six days more. Welcome her, that she may play her pretty games happy with old friends and may she often lisp my name. May the turf not be hard covering for her gentle bones and, Earth, rest not heavy on her; she was not heavy on thee."

Eheu fugaces, Postume, Postume, writes Horace to an old friend in an ode which begins with the most famous sigh in literature and ends with a wistful vision, exquisite in its pathos, of the remorselessness of death. It is the Roman version of the parable of the Rich Fool.

" Ah, Postumus, Postumus, the years slip by and all your piety cannot stay the wrinkles on the face, the coming of old age and of Death, which no man ever withstood; not though with countless sacrifice every day that flies you implore the remorseless god . . . we must all, all who live on the fruit of the earth, sail that last sea, whether we be kings or the poorest of hinds. In vain we shall keep from the bloody hand of war, in vain we shall keep from the heaving, angry sea, in vain we shall shield our bodies the autumn long from the fever-laden wind. The day will come when we must look on the creeping stream of Death's dark river. . . . You must leave your land, your home, your well-loved wife, and of your fondly-tended trees none but the deathly cypress shall go with its short-lived lord. Your heir with worthier lips than yours shall drain the Caecuban vintage you guarded by a hundred keys and its new proud lord shall drench the very floor with wine such as pontiff's banquets have not known."

And these are the words with which Tacitus concludes his biography of his father-in-law Agricola, the conqueror of Britain:

" If there be any place for the spirits of good men; if, as philosophers hold, the soul does not perish with the body, then is Agricola at rest, bidding his kindred put aside weak sorrow and unmanly grief and think of his noble life.   This we cannot lament or mourn; it is not meet.   Rather we should pay him our tribute in admiration and unmeasured praise and, if nature grant it, by moulding ourselves in his likeness.   This is the true piety, this the true homage of his kin.   To his daughter and his wife I would say, ' Honour his memory by weighing his words and actions in your hearts; hold to you the semblance not of his body, but of his soul.'   Not that I would set a ban on statues of marble or of bronze; yet faces, whether it be in flesh or in stone, are poor, perishable things; the soul's beauty lives for ever.   That beauty you may keep and set forth, not in stone by calling in the sculptor's art, but by your own living in the lineaments of your own life.   All that we loved in Agricola, all that we admired lives and will live, so long as time shall endure, in the minds of men and in the story of their deeds. Many of the great men of old lie buried in oblivion as though their fame and glory had never been. Agricola's story will be told to all posterity.   He will remain."

CHAPTER V

THE APPARATUS OF PRIVATE LIFE

Auream quisquis mediocritatem
diligit, tutus caret obsoleti
sordibus tecti, caret invidenda
sobrius aula.—HORACE.

" He who loves the Golden Mean lives safe from the squalor of crumbling walls and free from the envy that a palace brings."

HOUSES

THE story of the Roman house and how it developed from the primitive peasant hut into the familiar house of classical times can be traced with some accuracy. The first Roman " house " was a round hut with wall of wattle and clay and a thatched roof in which there was a hole to let out the smoke. The Romans, proud of their simple origins, for long took care to preserve show-specimens of such a hut, " the hut of Romulus," on the Palatine and Capitoline hills, as pious tokens of the past. And the type survives for us in the numerous burial-urns fashioned in the likeness of these huts which have been unearthed by the archaeologists. Such a hut is the direct ancestor of the essential constituent of the Roman house, which was a collection of rooms grouped round the central *atrium* or living-room (the word is thought to mean " the smoke-blackened room "), with an opening in the roof.

We shall consider only the essential types; but houses in the mass varied greatly. Rich men would have sumptuous and comfortable houses in town and country

86

alike. The poor frequently lived in tenement blocks such as we find in cities today. Between these extremes the middle-class Romans would live in houses much of the type which we shall describe. In the country would be found the simple huts of the peasants which changed little through the centuries and the rich villas set in great parks.

Let us look at houses which can be seen today in the

" House of the Surgeon " at Pompeii (Fourth–Third Century B.C.).
1, Vestibule. 2, Atrium. 3, Impluvium. 4, Ala. 5, Postern. 6, Tablinum.
7, Garden.

(Black lines show surviving parts of the house.)

ruins of Pompeii. Here, for example, is the " House of the Surgeon," the residence of a prosperous professional man.

Like most Roman houses, it is built round a central hall (*atrium*), roofed except for a small central opening (*compluvium*), which is directly over a shallow oblong basin (*impluvium*) sunk into the floor. The roof-tiling sloped inward on all sides to the *compluvium*, through which the rain-water would drain into the trough beneath. Round the *atrium* were grouped the living-rooms and bedrooms. At the farther end of the *atrium*, divided off by two wings (*alae*), is a group of three rooms with the main living-room (*tablinum*) or dining-room in the centre. The *tablinum* is open to the *atrium* on one side and to the garden behind on the other. This is an early house (it belongs to the third century B.C.), as its materials show; the front is of rough-dressed stone blocks, the other walls are of rubble within a framework of stone blocks; the floors are of beaten earth; the inside walls were plastered and decorated with a simple colour-wash.

In the " House of Pansa," dating from the second century B.C., we have a more luxurious type. This has beyond the *atrium* and the *tablinum* a square space with a pillared portico enclosing a garden and a fountain. Such a space was called by the Greek term *peristyle* (which means an enclosure with pillars round it). Leading off the peristyle in this house are again many rooms, such as would be required for a large household with many slaves. Beyond the peristyle again is a large garden. Round the house on three sides are shops, which, it has been suggested, would serve to insulate the house from the noises of the streets.

Thus the typical Roman house looked inward on to a hollow square, a plan calculated to give coolness in the hot summer days. The *atrium* was a spacious hall, in summer a place sharply divided between sunshine and shadow, as the sun beat sharply down through the opening in the roof. On wet days the rain would spout down the tiles and fall with spatter and splash into the *impluvium* beneath. In the *atrium* the clients would collect in the morning to wait for the master of the house

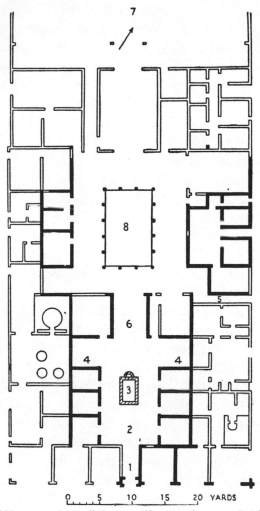

"HOUSE OF PANSA," POMPEII (SECOND CENTURY B.C.).
1, Vestibule. 2, Atrium. 3, Impluvium. 4, Ala. 5, Postern. 6, Tablinum.
7, Garden. 8, Peristyle.
(Black lines show surviving parts.)
Scale in yards.

to appear for the morning levée.   In the *alae* passages
were kept the death-masks of the family's ancestors and

the record of the family tree. In the *tablinum* the master
of the house kept his money and his papers; behind its
curtains he could work or talk with his friends or take
his siesta in peace. On the other side, if he wanted it,
was the brighter privacy of the peristyle with its flowers
and aromatic shrubs and perhaps the gentle whisper of
a fountain. He had but to draw back the curtain on
that side and he had all that to look on and enjoy.
Down in the colonnade on one side doors opened into
the dining-room and the kitchens.

The older house, such as the House of the Surgeon
with its rubble stone-faced walls, was a one-story house.
With the introduction of the new building methods of
concrete faced with brick it was possible to build
further stories. Upper rooms would be built round the
atrium and the peristyle. Staircases would appear, and
inner galleries running round the *atrium*. Outside rooms
could have balconies overhanging the street.

In Rome, too, would have been found, in residential quarters, on the Palatine, Quirinal and
Esquiline, private houses of the Pompeian types. But
these were for the wealthy. Most of Rome, the lower
and middle classes, by the end of republican times,
lived in apartments in big brick tenement houses, four
or five stories high. Once adequate building materials
were available, this development was inevitable in a
city where space became precious. Thus a street in
Rome would have looked much like a modern town
street, tall buildings on either side, except that roadways
were narrower. These crowded tenements were not
always very substantial in their top stories and were in
constant danger from fire and collapse; Augustus accordingly set a height-limit of seventy feet, which was later

reduced by Trajan to sixty. We can best see this city-type of house at Ostia, where recent excavations have revealed well-built and close-set houses still standing two stories high, with shops at the ground level on the outside, balconies to some of the upper rooms, and, in a few instances, an inner court on which the inside rooms face.

Inside decoration ranged from the simple colour-wash of the House of the Surgeon to elaborate stucco-reliefs, many-tinted dados and friezes. Sometimes tapestries were hung on the walls; sometimes pictures such as we frame and hang on our walls were painted and framed in paint on the wall-plaster, scenes from mythology and history predominating.

Windows were shuttered openings rather than the glass expanses to which we are used; transparent glazing materials were coming into use in the first century A.D., though we find Seneca classing them with silver taps as unnecessary luxuries (see p. 177).

For furniture there were chairs and couches in many forms, of wood, iron and bronze, usually furnished with coverlets and cushions of varying degrees of magnificence, the arms and feet carved more or less elaborately according to the wealth and taste of the owner.   In convenient places, often in the dining-room, would be built-in benches and couches of stone. Tables were made of all sorts of woods, built frequently to show off the grain. Vases and pots came to be used for ornament as well as for use.   In the rich man's house there would be many statues and statuettes in marble and bronze. Lamps were, of course, an indispensable article of furniture and of many forms and sizes.   An interesting selection may be seen in the British Museum. They ranged from the humble lamps of terra cotta as simple as a cottage candlestick to highly-adorned bronze pedestal lamps like the standard lamps of our drawing-rooms.

In place of carpets in the Roman house we must look for simple stone-paving or for mosaic, patterns made of small pieces of cut stone cemented together. Sometimes mosaics were severely symmetrical in black and white. Sometimes minute cubes of stone enamelled in all colours went to make up an elaborate picture. The famous mosaic of the Battle of Issus is 16 by 8 feet in size and made up of some 17,000 pieces.

For artificial lighting the house depended on lamps, some of which might have more than one wick, fed usually with olive-oil. For artificial heating small braziers containing charcoal embers could be moved from room to room. Rich houses might enjoy a primitive type of central heating, in that certain rooms might be heated from below by a furnace whose heat circulated under a floor raised on little pillars of tiling and came up through concealed shafts round the walls. Large houses had rooms specially built to catch the sun, as they had others designed for coolness and shade. For water-supply, there were always slave-women who could take a water-pot to the nearest well or public conduit; but the rich house might tap the public water-lines with lead pipes of its own. And, though Roman houses lacked many of the domestic comforts which modern plumbing and engineering have made possible for us, common sense provided them with many strangely modern-looking appliances, as the pedestal wash-basin of Delos and the latrines of the Roman fort at Housesteads will show. For kindling flint and tinder were used, and the early Empire even saw sulphur matches coming into common use and sold at street corners.   For time-keeping there were sundials and here and there a water-clock working on the principle of the familiar hour-glass.   The minor furniture, the hundred and one little articles of domestic routine, scissors, knives, spoons, cooking vessels, buckets, brushes and brooms, tweezers, pins, brooches, locks, keys, hair-pins, combs—have not greatly varied from ancient to modern times.   They may be seen in almost any museum attached to a Roman site and in abundance in such collections as that of the British Museum.

COUNTRY HOUSES

The country cottage was, as we have seen, in its simplest form a one-roomed hut of wood, wattle and straw, perhaps sometimes of rough stone.   Just as the town house was in essence simply such a hut with excrescences, so in essence the farm-house or *villa* was a number of such huts arranged for the purposes of convenience or defence round the central farmyard.   From this beginning developed the country-house architecture of wealthier times.

Overleaf is a villa built in the first century B.C., between Pompeii and Boscoreale in central Italy.   It consists of a courtyard round which on three sides runs a colonnade. On the north lie the master's quarters and the main living-rooms; on the other two sides are the out-houses used for the daily work of the estate.

FOOD

It is safe to say that there can have been no great difference between the food of the ancient Roman and that native to Italy today.   Corn and flour from wheat; the vine; the olive; the abundant vegetables (beans,

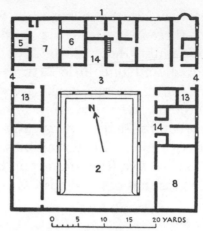

VILLA NEAR BOSCOREALE.

1, Owner's Quarters. 2, Courtyard. 3, Portico. 4, Entrance. 5, Slaves' Quarters. 6, Bath. 7, Kitchen. 8, Stable. 13, Door-keeper's Room. 14, Domestic Shrine.

(Black lines show surviving parts.)

Scale in yards.

peas, cabbages, artichokes, cucumber, onions, garlic, fennel, lettuce, radishes; apples, peaches, pears, apricots, figs, melons, plums)—all were there, as were the flocks and herds which gave the Italian his meat, his milk and his cheese, and the fowls and wild birds and small game. There were his bees to provide him with the ancient equivalent of sugar. Lastly there were the seas to give him his fish: mullet, tunny, turbot, anchovy and the rest.

Breakfast was a hasty affair: a piece of bread with honey or salt to give it a taste or perhaps dipped in wine or with a handful of olives and raisins. Lunch was a more serious meal, with eggs, or meat, vegetables or salad, fruit and cheese; but dinner (*cena*) was the important meal of the day. Dinner consisted in the main of three courses: an *hors d'oeuvres* course which would commonly include eggs, preserved and spiced fish and vegetables in various combinations and disguises; a main course of meats, game and vegetables; and a dessert, cakes and fruit and nuts. Wine appropriate to each course would be served. We are constantly reading in Latin literature of the extravagances of the rich man's table; we must remember that they are extravagances (it is commonly the unusual things, not the normal, which get the headlines) and not take our cue from them. If we are to form an impression of normal life, let us think rather of two menus which the modest Martial offers:

I. Hors d'oeuvres of chopped leeks, tunny-fish, egg.
_____

Bacon and beans.
Sausage and spelt-mash.
Cabbage.
_____

Grapes. Pears. Toasted chestnuts.

II. Mallows, salad of mint, leeks, eruca.
Chopped eggs with shell-fish flavoured with rue.
Middle-cut of tunny.
_____

Roast kid.
Chicken. Ham.
Beans. Sprouts.
_____

Apples.
Conversation to taste ad lib.

It is interesting to note that the second menu compensates for its more ambitious main course by providing the simplest of dessert.

For a dinner-party the conventional arrangement was of three couches, each with three places, round three sides of a square. Tables were small and such as the servants could bring in or out. Consequently much of the food was served in a form which required little service once it was brought in. Spoons might be used, but knives were rarely used at table, and there were no forks. Fingers were freely used. This naturally gave importance to napkins, which might be elaborately bordered or fringed and of fine materials according to the taste of the owner; for each guest brought his own. Catullus in one of his poems condemns the bad taste of a fellow-guest who thought it funny to filch other people's napkins at a dinner-party. As the couches were comfortably cushioned and the guests reclined at ease throughout the meal instead of sitting, there was no need to migrate to study or drawing-room when the meal was over; the evening could be comfortably spent in the one room, whether conversation was the order of the day or whether the host provided musicians and dancing-girls for his guests' entertainment. At a normal dinner-party the host's wife and possibly other members of the family might be present for the meal, and even stay on after the dessert.

Breakfast was, of course, taken soon after rising but might be postponed until the master had held his morning reception of clients in the *atrium*. The day was divided into twelve hours, between sunrise and sunrise, which would vary in length according to the time of year; noon was a fixed point coinciding with the end of the sixth hour. By the close of the second hour the morning reception would be over; business in the City began about the third hour. The dinner (*cena*) in early times had been at midday, but with the increase in public business came to be postponed to late afternoon or early evening. In the early Empire *prandium* (lunch) was eaten about noon and followed by a siesta, the length of which depended on the habits and interests of the

PLATE XI.—PERISTYLE OF THE HOUSE OF THE MYSTERIES, POMPEII.

To the right is seen the main entrance.

PLATE XII.—WINE-PRESS IN THE HOUSE OF THE
MYSTERIES, POMPEII.

Note, on the left, the channel down which the new wine flows from the
press.

individual. The afternoon was, for those who wanted it, the time for games and exercise and for visiting the Baths (a lengthy affair as with our modern Turkish baths and offering in the process most of the amenities of a Club). Dinner came about the ninth or the tenth hour and, in company, might last indefinitely as with us.

The diet of the common people can be fairly well imagined from what has been said. The Romans were not great meat-eaters, and the basis of ordinary eating was given by vegetables, bread and the porridge or mush made of spelt. The farmer in the " Moretum " (a short poem which used to be ascribed to Virgil), who gets up in the early morning to make himself a good breakfast before going out to hard work in the fields, makes himself a good tasty salad; and the soldier who had to go on a meat ration when corn ran short thought himself hard done to. As for drink, everyone reckoned to drink wine of a sort, however tart and villainous to an educated palate the cheapest sorts might be.

CLOTHES

The normal everyday dress for both men and women in all grades of society was the *tunica*, a simple short-sleeved shirt or chemise usually of wool, reaching just below the knees. A girdle might be worn through which it could be hitched up to give greater freedom of movement. Ordinarily this was all the Roman wore as he went about the house or about his work, unless his work was of a public, formal nature. For formal occasions the citizen wore (over his *tunica*) the toga. In essence this was a large woollen shawl draped over the left shoulder till one end touched the feet, the rest being carried round the back, under the right armpit, across the chest and over the left shoulder to fall once more to the heel. The right arm was thus left free. There was plenty of material to form folds, and the fold across the breast could be used as the equivalent of a pocket. As it developed, the toga became wider and more voluminous with tapering ends. It was a graceful, dignified garment and, though it might be deplored on occasion as unwieldy and uncomfortable (as ʹall formal dress comes to be deplored), it was the badge of Roman citizenship, and Virgil can write with pride:

Romanos, rerum dominos gentemque togatam.
("... Romans, the lords of the earth, the toga'd brood.")[1]

The tunics and togas of plain ordinary people would keep the natural colour of the wool, dull cream, grey or brown. As time went on, finer materials were used. Gentlemen wore white and, in particular, a candidate for public office took care to parade a toga of conspicuous whiteness; hence the name *candidatus*. But the dull hues were worn in mourning or by anyone who considered himself under a cloud, for example on trial in the law-courts, or wished to mark his sympathy with a friend who might be in similar trouble. Senators were distinguished by a tunic which had a broad purple stripe down the middle; members of the equestrian order by a narrow stripe of the same sort. The higher magistrates and priests wore a purple band on the edge of the toga (the *toga praetextata*); so did boys till they came of age and put on the plain toga of manhood. In all these instances the stripe was originally in all probability a charm against the evil eye, a power to which

[1] Or, as Dr. T. R. Glover observed to me, " they are the masters; you see them everywhere—*but not in uniform.*"

children (because they were weaker than grown-up people) and holders of high office (because they were more conspicuous) would be thought especially susceptible. Emperors came to assume the privilege of wearing an all-purple toga; hence " assuming the purple " became a familiar synonym for " becoming emperor." It should be added that in hue " purple " was nearer what we should call red.

The feminine equivalent of the toga (a woman who wore the toga branded herself as " fast ") was the *stola*, which was a longer and more elaborate form of the *tunica* and was, indeed, sometimes called the *tunica exterior*. It reached to the feet and was worn with a girdle through which it could be pulled up to fall in graceful folds. Matrons wore a *stola* with a flounce round the bottom hem. Materials here gave abundant scope for variety (linen from Egypt, silks and cottons from the East came in to supplement the original wool), as did the metal and jewelled clasps which might be used to adjust the draping of the bodice. In later imperial times fashion came to substitute a more graceful long-sleeved garment called a *dalmatica* (the name and the style survives in the vocabulary of ecclesiastical vesture), which was even adopted by men. Out of doors a light mantle called the *palla* was worn over the *stola*, with a fold of it draped over the head.

For warmth more than one tunic could be worn (the Emperor Augustus, who had a weak chest and suffered from colds, is said to have worn as many as four). Invalids and travellers in cold regions might wear leg-wrappings (somewhat after the fashion of puttees). And there were cloaks of many kinds. The *lacerna* was a light sleeveless cape, secured on the shoulder or breast with a brooch, the *laena* a rather heavier cloak serving as the normal great-coat; both were worn in all colours. The *paenula* was a large, thick garment, of frieze or felt or even of leather, which could be worn by both men and women, for travelling in wet or cold weather, a sort of ulster; it might have a hood attached, in which case it was called *cucullus*, the ancestor of the cowled habit of the monk.

Head-dress was little used. Against a sudden shower the outer garment could usually be pulled over the head; but for outdoor workers there was the *pilleus*, the pointed felt cap, and for travellers the broad-brimmed *petasus* for protection against the sun.

For foot-wear the standard was the sandal *solea*, which in its simplest form was a sole with strappings to keep it firm round ankle and foot. The *calceus* was a more substantial shoe, made of soft leather and completely covering the foot, fastened in front with thongs. This was the normal full-dress shoe worn with the toga or the palla. Senators wore a calceus of black leather with its thongs tied round the ankle and lower calf, and adorned on the instep with an ornament of crescent-shaped ivory. Soldiers and countrymen wore the *caliga*, a heavy sandal with a hob-nailed sole. Slippers of various shapes and colours (*socci*) were worn about the house, sandals when one went out to dinner, but proper shoes were the really respectable wear for the street. Women's shoes were much the same as men's, but finer and more brightly coloured.

HAIR

In the early days of the Republic shaggy hair and beards were the Roman fashion for men, until under

Hellenic influence the Roman became a man of the world and found that in the civilized world one shaved. *Barbati illi* (" the bearded ones ") became a household expression for the remote ancestors who lived in the days when Romans were farmers; one may compare the zeal with which modern South Africans grow beards to qualify for a share in the Voortrekker celebrations. From the middle of the second century B.C. portrait busts show beardless faces and neat-trimmed hair, until the beginning of the second century A.D., when the Emperor Hadrian reintroduced the beard, which recommended itself to him as the symbol of the Greek philosopher. Women kept their hair long, but dyes and elaborate coiffures, as can be seen in the portrait busts of the Empire, came to be used as commonly as they are today.

Jewelry of all sorts was worn and has survived—rings, brooches, armlets, bracelets, earrings, anklets, pendants, hair-nets of finely-meshed gold—in profusion. Nor has archaeology failed to reveal the powder-bowls and scent-bottles of the Roman lady's dressing-table, and cosmetic apparatus no less elaborate than that of her modern counterpart, the dark blue eye-shading and the rouge still red in the jar.

CHAPTER VI

ROME AT WORK

Nil sine magno
vita labore dedit mortalibus.—HORACE.

" Life never gave anything to mortal man without hard work."

" WHY is it," Horace asks in the opening lines of his first Satire, " that nobody is content with his own way of life, with the calling which he has chosen or fortune has thrown in his way ? why must we always be sighing for another man's work ? ' Lucky fellows who can be merchants,' says the old service-worn soldier. ' The army's the place,' says the merchant at sea, in the grip of a nasty South-easter; ' over the top, and it's all over, one way or the other, in a twinkling.' The lawyer, knocked up before cock-crow by some client hammering on his door, is all for the farmer's life. Your farmer, hauled up from the country to attend in court, swears that only townfolk get any peace."

Soldier, merchant, farmer, lawyer; it is an interesting selection and no doubt representative. Since an anatomy of all trades is manifestly impossible, we might do worse than follow Horace's cue.

THE FARMER

We will begin with the land; for though in imperial times Italian agriculture came to play a very subdued part in the economies of empire, in the early days it had been the bedrock of Roman life and worth. With the coming of the great wars and the extension of Rome's dominion and interests, the old small-scale agriculture had waned before the encroachment of big business. The small-holder could no longer fight Rome's battles and at the same time attend to his farm. He stayed with the legions and when wars were over drifted to Rome to pick up his living there and to receive the dole. Farms went to decay, and the long skirmishing Second Punic War, with Hannibal at large in Italy, must in many regions have put an end to the old settled farm-life; and then the big business man stepped in, buying out impoverished small-holders and taking over derelict farms and so forming huge ranches on which he could speculate in sheep-rearing on a large scale. Given plenty of pasture and cheap labour (slaves were cheap in the age of the great wars), sheep-rearing involved comparatively few overhead charges and was vastly more profitable than corn-growing, which requires more equipment, more intensive labour and more skill. Corn-growing declined. Once the fields round Rome had provided all the corn Rome needed; now Rome's corn came from Sardinia and Sicily, from Africa, Spain and, above all, from Egypt. Nor were there any tariffs to protect the home farmer; the Empire remained a free-trade world to the end.

Yet the Roman State was in its first beginnings a commonwealth of farmers worthy of the name. Though farming fell on evil days, the Romans still liked to think that their ancestors were working sons of the soil; that the messengers who brought word to Cincinnatus that he had been elected Dictator found him at his plough. Under Augustus the government did all it could to encourage this sentiment, and a great Back to the Land movement was started in which the services of the best

poets of the day played a memorable part. Not that
there had been any danger of country life dying out.
There were always the vineyards and oliveyards which
still make Italy the garden of Europe, and the country
estate was still the highest esteemed form of property.

The poets of the Augustan age are full of the praises of
the countryside, and there are similar passages in prose.
Cicero in his treatise on Old Age makes Cato remark on
the attractions of country produce:

> " The good and careful owner can always show a
> full wine-cellar, oil-store and granary; the farmhouse
> is never at a loss for pork, kid, lamb, poultry, milk,
> cheese, honey.   And then there is the garden which
> the farmer calls his second larder.   Bird-snaring and
> hunting in his leisure hours can make this fare still
> more savoury.   And need I speak of the satisfaction
> of green meadows, the trees all in a row, the beauty of
> the vineyard and olive grove ? "

That was old Cato seen through literary·spectacles.
The real Cato was more practically-minded.   He wrote
a Farmer's Handbook from which we can learn more
concrete information.   The farm of 100 *iugera* (about
66 acres), he tells us, should consist of a good vineyard,
with elms up which the vines can be trained, a garden
capable of being irrigated, an osier bed (for cutting
withies for building and fencing), an olive-orchard, a
field for grain, an orchard, an acorn grove and a bit of
woodland for timber.   It should have sound farm-
buildings, plenty of room in the oil-cellars and wine-vats
and a good supply of storage-casks, in case you want to
keep your stuff till prices are better.

On another page he describes the ideal olive-farm of

160 acres. The labour required is: bailiff and house-keeper (these would be well-tried slaves), five ordinary labourers, three ox-drivers, one ass-driver, one shepherd. For live-stock would be needed three yoke of oxen, three asses with panniers, an ass for the mill and a hundred sheep. The bailiff, he adds, must be up first in the morning and the last to bed; the housekeeper must not be one to waste her time gossiping, but must keep the house well swept and look after the poultry and the eggs and the making of preserves. The normal fare for the labourers is barley-meal, bread, figs, olives, pickles, vinegar, salt and wine. Their clothing is to be doled out on a strict allowance. There follows much else; instructions for the upkeep of live-stock and waggons, for vintage and olive-crop, recipes and homely remedies for human and other ailments, a curious blend of super-stition and common sense.

We may supplement this outline with a few lines about such a farm by the poet Martial, writing at the end of the first century A.D.:

> No landscape-gardener's ordered whim
> Of shaven hedge and myrtles trim,
> No pleasaunce cumbering fertile ground,
> But hearty Country raw and sound. . . .
> In every nook good grain is stored
> And wine from many an Autumn's hoard. . . .
>
> About the crowded farmyard wander
> Jewelled peacock, hissing gander;
> Pheasant, partridge, flamingo
> In brilliant plumage come and go;
> Proud Rhodian cockerels seek the hen;
> While from all sides in high-set cotes,
> Rustle of wings and coo of throats,
> Pigeon and dove unceasing call;
> The farm-wife's apron holds in thrall

The greedy porkers; here the lamb
Awaits the filled udder of its dam.
And baby slaves bask in the light
Where peaceful hearth burns high and bright. . . .

Of the cultivation of grain little need be said. It was of the primitive type familiar to us from the pages of the New Testament, and many of the old processes can still be seen in the plains of Italy today. The plough was of wood throughout and simple enough in its construction to be home-made (Virgil, in his *Georgics*—" The Farmer's Handbook "—gives instructions for making it), and drawn by oxen. The usual crop was of wheat, sown in October, reaped in May and June. Reaping was done with the sickle, threshing with the flail, or by the trampling feet of oxen, and the winnowing-fan. We note that Cato, in his description of the small farm, mentions only a solitary cornfield, and we may take it that for the most part the small farmer grew corn only for his own consumption. It would be stored and ground a little at a time as required in small stone mills turned by hand.

Hand in hand with corn goes wine. The grape, like the olive early introduced from Greece, became the great Italian product. Vineyards might be on the level, but were preferably on southward-facing slopes. They were grown in serried rows, as today, propped on trellises or on single wooden props or on elms, kept specially small by cutting. Vintage came in September or October. The grapes were gathered and carried in baskets to the vats, where they were trod by naked feet to a juicy pulp. The pulp went to the wine-press, from which the juice was drained into great store-jars which were stored half-buried in earth for coolness. These were left uncovered for a few days till a certain stage in the fermentation was reached; then the wine was drawn off into smaller jars and stored away for the owner's use or for despatch in the way of trade.

There were many varieties of Italian wine, the most famous those of the west coast, the Massic, the Caecuban, the Falernian and the Formian. The grape was also eaten abundantly as fresh fruit, and portions of the harvest might be reserved for drying into raisins.

The third member of the triad was the olive. An oliveyard was a solemn investment; for an olive-tree takes nearly twenty years to come to full fruition and forty years to come to its best. But once planted it calls for very little attention beyond digging round the roots. Olives are small trees growing to thick gnarled trunks, not much bigger than willows, very beautiful in their shimmering leaves; these are a dark green on top, but in a breeze flash up their silvery undersides. Olive-harvest was from October to December, a laborious business; for the olives, like our hops, had to be picked carefully by hand. After picking the olives were left in heaps for a few days to mellow and then crushed in the olive-mill, a heavy stone mill turned by a donkey. The resultant pulp was then pressed; usually the first pressing yielded the best oil, which was used for food; the second pressing gave the oil used for the toilet; the third, burning-oil for lamps; the remaining refuse came in handy as fuel. Thus the olive, as has been observed, served a threefold need; it was the butter, the soap and the electric light of the ancient world.[1]

Lastly, as well as the great triad, corn, wine and olive, there was a great variety of fruits and vegetables: strawberries and cherries in spring; melons, apricots, peaches,

[1] See Zimmern, *Greek Commonwealth*, p. 50.

plums in summer; pears, apples and figs in autumn; and, among other vegetables, beans, turnips, peas, artichokes, cabbages, onions, garlic and spinach. These would be grown on a small scale and, in the days before the invention of refrigerative and canning processes made it possible to convey such perishables in long-distance trade, mainly for home consumption.

There are interesting glimpses of farm-life in Virgil's first *Georgic*. Here is a passage about the odd jobs always to be done about a farm:

> " When winter rains keep the countryman indoors, there are many things he may do at leisure, things that else he will have to do hastily on fine days. The ploughman can beat out the point of a blunted share; wooden vats can be hollowed out; sheep can be marked; and grain-sacks numbered; stakes can be sharpened and fork-end props and willow-slips made ready for fastening up vines. Rainy days too are the days for weaving baskets from briar-twigs, for parching your corn by the fire, for grinding your flour. Even on holy days there are little tasks to be done without offence to man or God; there is no commandment against watering your fields, against fencing your cornland, snaring birds, burning brambles, or dipping your flocks in the good stream. On such days the driver may load his ass with oil and common apples and bring back with him from the town it may be a new mill-stone or a lump of pitch."

And here is a passage of advice about times and seasons, practical no doubt, but instinct too with the poet's excitement in the very counterchange of day and night, in the mysteries of summer and winter.

> " Much too there is better done in the cool of night

or at sundawn, when the dew is thick upon the fields.
Night is the time to cut stubble; night is the time for
mowing a dry meadow, when the dew is on it.   One
man I know sits late by the winter fire to cut and
sharpen his torches, while his wife sings at her work
beside him, as she plies the ringing comb at her loom
or boils down the sweet new wine over the fire and
skims the bubbling surface with a leaf.   But hot noon
is the time to cut the brown corn and for treading out
the dry grain on the threshing-floor.   Strip to plough
and strip to sow; easy days come in the winter.   When
the cold days come the farmer can enjoy in peace the
good harvest he has gathered in. . . . Winter is the
time of good cheer. . . . Yet winter is the time, too,
to strip the acorns from the oak and the berries from
the laurel, the olive and the blood-red myrtle; to lay
snares for the crane and nets for the stag and chase
the long-eared hare . . . when snow lies deep and
rivers drive down ice.''

THE SOLDIER

We turn to the soldier.   The transition is easy, as the
Romans regarded themselves as much a martial as an
agricultural people.   It was the peasant soldiery, the
rusticorum mascula militum proles, of Horace's phrase, that
had made the name of Rome great.   This is not the
place to dilate on the history of the Roman army and
on the organization of its component units.   It will be
enough to say that the citizen militia of early republican
days had by the imperial age been transformed into a
professional army.   Some of the reasons for this change
we have seen and something, too, of the influence which
it brought to bear on the transformation of the Roman
State from Republic to Empire.   At the moment we
are concerned with more concrete aspects, above all

with the details which will enable us to form a picture of the soldier's life.

In the reign of Augustus the normal strength of the standing army was twenty-eight legions, spread out according to the various exigencies of frontier-garrisoning and other military needs throughout the provinces of the Empire. A legion was a division whose full strength was 6,000 men. Each legion was divided into ten cohorts of 600 men each, each cohort into six centuries of 100 men. It was officered by a *legatus* as C.O., six tribunes and sixty centurions.

These centurions were almost always men who had risen from the ranks and combined the long-tried experience of sergeant-majors with the authority of commissioned officers. On them the discipline and efficiency of the legion in practice depended. Under the Republic, when armies were either citizen-militias or levies raised on the initiative of individuals, when recruiting was largely a hand-to-mouth affair and disbandments sudden, there were no regimental histories. Under the Empire, when armies were divorced from politics and partisan allegiances and permanently attached to the central authority, legions were definite bodies which developed distinctive qualities and came to take pride in their records. Promotion became more regular and more comprehensive. In the old days the common soldier might rise to the centurionate, but there was little prospect of rising higher. Under the Empire, senior centurions might pass on into the equestrian grades of service and become eligible for the responsible administrative posts to which they led. These legions (only Roman citizens could enlist in them) constituted one half of the Roman army. The other half was composed of " auxiliaries," non-citizen forces officered in the main by citizens. The auxiliaries were recruited from a diversity of races, Gauls, Numidians, Cretans, Balearic islanders, Germans—and contributed most of the cavalry and other subsidiary arms, such as slingers and archers. They had to do much of the frontier police-work and in more serious fighting often had to bear the brunt, in order to save the legions. Normally the auxiliaries served for twenty-five years and on discharge received the citizenship.

The legionary normally served for twenty-five years, twenty with the colours, five as a veteran in separate detachments exempt from the normal fatigues of camp routine and constituting a special reserve. His pay was in our money about sixpence a day, that is rather over £8 a year, and out of this stoppages were made for food and clothing, so that it is unlikely that he received more than half his pay in cash. But there is good evidence that he could live comfortably on about two-thirds of his pay. And the existence of legionary savings-banks, which were a regular and compulsory feature of the imperial military system, suggests that soldiers could manage to save. It is estimated that about 60 modii of corn would keep a soldier for a year, and a modius usually cost one denarius (about $8\frac{1}{2}d$.). His fare was simple: corn or bread (corn need not always be ground and made into flour or bread; on active service he could content himself with roast or parched corn), vegetables, soup, lard, and for drink cheap wine or vinegar and water. Soldiers were not great meat-eaters and on occasion complained loudly when they could not get their corn and had to live on meat.

The legionary was a heavy-armed infantryman. For

uniform he wore a woollen tunic and over that a leather jerkin, reaching to the knee, reinforced round the torso and over the shoulders with metal bands and plates; a close-fitting short-crested helmet; a thick brown woollen cloak which would serve at need as a blanket; and heavy hobnailed sandals. In cold countries such as Britain he might wear leg-wrappings like our puttees or even breeches. He was close-shaved and had his hair cropped close to his head.

His arms consisted of a half-cylindrical shield some 4 feet long by 2½ feet wide made of leather with metal rim and a metal boss-spike in the middle; a broad two-edged stabbing 'sword not more than 2 feet long; the *pilum*, a throwing-spear consisting of a wooden shaft with a long 2-foot iron head, the whole measuring 6–7 feet in length (of these he usually carried two). The shield was carried on the left arm, the sword on a belt on the right side. Sometimes on his left side he would carry a dagger.

On the march he had to carry, in addition to his personal kit, entrenching tools and stakes for making camp-palisades, cooking-pot and rations. All this was made up into a manageable pack by the help of a wooden framework, invented by the famous general Marius, which had the advantage of distributing the weight on the shoulders and of enabling the soldier to put off his pack quickly without interfering with his armour.

Life in the Roman army was a matter of stern and fixed discipline, in battle, in camp, on the march. It is indicative of Roman order that a fixed system of march became a regulation as early as the second century B.C.: first the picked auxiliaries, then the auxiliary right wing

PLATE XIII.—MOSAIC PAVEMENT FROM THE HOUSE OF
CICERO, POMPEII.

Street musicians, wearing masks: a dancer with tambourine, accompanied by
a castanet-player and a woman playing a flute: an urchin looks on. A fine
piece of work signed by the artist in the top left-hand corner (in Greek—
"Dioscurides of Samos made this").

PLATE XIV.—OSTIA.

1. Mosaic pavement of a house.

2. The House of Diana—remains of a typical large apartment-house, divided into flats (date, second century A.D.).

followed by their baggage and that of the picked force (this would be transported in waggons); then the legions followed by their baggage, and the left allied wing preceded by their baggage brought up the rear. Such was the formation normally kept by any considerable force on the move. In dangerous country the march might be made in square formation with the baggage in the middle and two strong forces marching on the flanks. And, as a rule, no Roman army ever halted for the night without constructing a defensible camp with rampart and ditch. Camp-making, too, was a matter of great precision and followed strict regulations. The camp was square, entirely surrounded by a ditch, the upcast earth from which was heaped to form the rampart, which was topped with a palisade made from the stakes which every legionary carried. Two main roads intersecting at right angles crossed the camp, and right at the centre stood the general's headquarters. There was a gate at each end of the two roads. This plan survived in many towns which grew out of military camps and may be seen exemplified in the structure of Gloucester in this country, which was almost certainly at one time the camp of the Second Legion Augusta; its chief streets, intersecting as the streets of a Roman camp, are known as Northgate Street, Southgate Street, Eastgate Street and Westgate Street to this day. The camp was carefully guarded by relays of sentries and cavalry pickets night and day.

The order of battle naturally varied according to circumstances, but the formation known as the *triplex acies* and commonly used by Julius Caesar is typical. In this order the cohorts of a legion were drawn up in three lines, four cohorts in the first line and three in each of the other

8

two, so arranged that the rear lines covered the spaces left in front. First the cohorts of the front line went into action, hurling their *pila* and then using the sword hand to hand; if their charge was not decisive the cohorts of the second line came up into action as second wave through the spaces in the front line and engaged the enemy. In this way the two front lines shared the attack, while the third constituted a defence in their rear. The cavalry did not as a rule play a prominent part; it was used to screen the flanks, to check any skirmishing movements by the enemy's horse and, above all else, for pursuit after a successful engagement. It was not in the best period of Rome used for shock frontal tactics against the enemy's main body, as it had been used by Alexander in the past and was to be used by Belisarius in the future.

Finally, a word about siege-operations. Preferring as they did to take their objectives, whether towns or strongholds, by storm rather than by blockade, the Romans had many ingenious devices of siegecraft. They battered at the walls with a great, swinging iron-nosed beam which they called a ram, protecting its operators with sheds and mantlets; they built up causeways sloping at an easy gradient to the top of the wall; they dug mines and galleries to penetrate under the walls; they built high towers on wheels to overtop the walls, so that they could fire down on the defenders and let men down by gangways within the wall; they advanced up to the wall with their shields locked above their heads in the formation known as the *testudo* (" the tortoise "); they had an elaborate repertoire of artillery. There was the *ballista*, a heavy machine operated by the high tension of ropes or gut to hurl stone shot of any

weight up to 500 pounds a distance of between 500 and
1,000 feet, dropping it down in a curved trajectory, like a
modern howitzer.   There was the *onager* (" the kicker "),
a smaller machine and therefore more mobile, working
on the same principle.   Then there was the arrow-
engine, the *catapulta*, which worked like the cross-bow,
shooting a heavy arrow, with the greater precision possible in a flat trajectory, up a groove over a far greater
range.   Living in the era of gunpowder, in the age of
high explosive, we must beware of belittling the skill and
science with which this ancient torsion artillery was
worked.   In ancient military literature we find hints
which will win the respect of all generations of modern
gunners.   We find in the pages of Vitruvius, an engineer who served in Africa under Julius Caesar, the
remark that a good gunner should have a good ear for
music; for, if the two driving ropes of his machine are
not so twisted as to sound the same note, it will not shoot
accurately.   The same writer gives elaborate dimen-
sions and proportions for both flat and curved trajectory
artillery.   Indeed the mathematics of ballistics had
been worked out in the third century B.C. by one Hero,
a Greek of Alexandria.

Order was the watchword of the Roman army, as of
so much else that was Roman.   The Roman soldier was
above all a man trained to obey orders, and trained to
obey orders in all departments of service.   " You see
now," says Cicero, in one of his essays, " you see now
why we call our army *exercitus*.   It knows the meaning
of exercise to the full.   Take the strain of a route march;
the men carry more than a fortnight's rations, not to
mention rampart stakes and personal kit.   As for shield,
sword, helmet, our men count them no more part of

their pack than they count their shoulders, arms and hands. A soldier's weapons they reckon parts of his body; they get so used to the feel of them that when the moment comes they can throw down their packs and fight with their weapons as free and unencumbered as though they were limbs. Consider, too, the training the legions go through, the strain of advancing at the double, the charge, the battle-cry. This is what makes the spirit which in action is ready for any wound. Compare an untrained man with a trained soldier, given equal courage; beside the other he will look like a woman. What makes the difference, the difference which experience has proved to be there, between veterans and recruits? The recruit may have the advantage of youth, but it is only habit which teaches men to stand under strain and to disregard wounds."

We have still extant some interesting and strangely modern inspection reports issued by the Emperor Hadrian in the beginning of the second century A.D. after reviews of various units serving in Africa, of which the following is a specimen. It is remarkably like the speeches which inspecting officers make to O.T.C. contingents in our English schools.

To the First Pannonian Squadron

"You were quick to obey orders and you manoeuvred well over the whole ground. Your javelin-throwing was accurate and good, and that although the javelins were of a type difficult to grasp. Your spear-throwing, too, was in many cases excellent, and the jumping was neat and lively. I would certainly have pointed out to you anything in which you were deficient if I had noticed it; for example, if you had shown a tendency to overshoot your targets. But there has been no flaw of any kind. All your exercises have been performed absolutely according to rule."

The above statement was made to an auxiliary unit attached to the legion III Augusta stationed in the province of Africa. Its mention will serve as a reminder that the Roman soldier by no means spent all his days in campaigning, in marches and battles. He would also be a real civilizing force in the country in which he was quartered. Trade and something more than trade followed the imperial flag, and round the legionary depots in many provinces grew up flourishing civil settlements. Old soldiers when they retired from the colours might find it hard to leave the land in which they had spent the best part of their lives, and many of them settled down with their wives as peaceful citizens in places where they would still be in touch with their old comrades and, as such, could be a good example to the native population. In quiet provinces rendered secure by his presence, notably in Africa and Syria, the soldier who was still serving became semi-civilian. The army atmosphere was essentially Roman, and whether the soldier was a native Italian or not he became the embodiment of Roman language and manners, law and ideas and the instrument by which all these took root among the provincials. The history of legion III Augusta is a striking instance of this civilizing power. At the beginning of the imperial age Roman Africa was one of the most backward regions of the Empire; in the third century A.D. it was one of the most progressive (it gave the world the great Christian writers Tertullian and Saint Augustine of Hippo); the development was due very largely to the continued presence of legion III Augusta.   Roads, milestones and the magnificent ruins of Timgad, a city of tawny African marble in the midst of the Saharan sands, provide to this day its eloquent memorial.

Si pacem vis habere para bellum (" if you want peace, be ready for war ") is an aphorism which in our day has assumed a gigantic significance.   But whatever the rights and wrongs of its application to the modern problem of armaments, its validity as an expression of military policy under the Roman Empire is indisputable. On this point we may take note of a remarkable passage written by Hero of Alexandria in his manual on gun construction:

> " The greatest and most essential part of the study of philosophy is that which treats of tranquillity of mind.   This always has been, still is and probably will always be the chief concern of the philosophy. Yet mechanics can claim a still higher place; for this science, merely by one of its incidental applications, shows men how they may live in tranquillity.   I refer to the branch which deals with gun construction. The philosophy which is implied in the appliances with which it is concerned ensures security in peace and war.   For this reason its study deserves continual encouragement.   Even in time of complete peace it should be encouraged; for by it we may hope to make peace more enduring, we can set our own minds at rest by confidence in the thought that we are prepared, and potential enemies, observing our preparedness, will be slow to venture an attack.   But if the art is neglected, and due preparation is not made, even the smallest quarrel may have the most serious consequences."

Horace and Cicero, having lived in the horrors of civil war, might stress the wounds and the discomforts of the soldier's life; but in the imperial age, taken all round, there was not much fighting. Once the boundaries of Empire had been fixed, the Roman army was too good to admit of it. The legions were posted round the outside of the Empire, not indeed on its edge (for there the auxiliaries bore the brunt), and such wars as troubled the Roman Peace were border raids rather than serious military incursions. Thus the legions tended to become residential garrison armies in permanent stations. In such conditions legionaries might at times grow slovenly, as they tended to become in Syria, that hot-house of Eastern sophistication (there were veterans there in the time of Corbulo, says Tacitus, who had never been on guard and looked on ramparts and trenches as novelties), but they were the exception to point the rule. The armies of the West were always disciplined; constantly revising their tactics and equipment and building with Roman strength and thoroughness to the end of Roman times.

The Merchant

The merchant we must see in Horace's eyes as an indefatigable voyager after gain:

> *impiger extremos curris mercator ad Indos,*
> *per mare pauperiem fugiens, per saxa, per ignes.*

" Restless merchant scouring the globe to farthest Ind,
Through sea, through rocks, through fire running from penury. . . ."

He is not a high-class Roman. Senators were forbidden to traffic in commerce; the Claudian Law of 218 B.C. prohibited them from owning ships except for the purpose of conveying the produce of their own estates, and so for the most part they kept to real estate

and shareholding in joint stock companies. Thus commerce remained largely in the hands of the aristocracy
of wealth and, in its smaller concrete aspects, in the hands
of Greeks and orientals (yet these Greeks, we must
remember, were in the larger sense Roman and served
the world of Rome).

Our merchant, then, is a Greek with his warehouses
at Puteoli, or a Syrian settled in Alexandria, or a Jew
of Antioch, or a freed man from a wealthy Roman's
country estate who has scraped together enough savings
to buy his liberty and a part-share in a trading-ship.
Normally the *mercator* is also a ship-owner, voyaging with
his cargo and therefore, as the poets make clear, constantly exposed to the perils of the deep. Compared
with the modern trader he shows a balance of dis-
advantage. For ships were small and at the mercy of
contrary winds (which is why sailing-ships remained
small till the invention in comparatively modern times
of fore-and-aft rigging), with sailing practicable during
a bare seven months of the year. What happened to
the skipper who put out to sea when the sailing season
was over we know from the account of Saint Paul's
voyage in the closing chapters of Acts, and from the
many epigrams and epitaphs they have left us. " Ill-
starred Nicanor," runs a poignant epigram of the
Roman period written by a Greek of Thessalonica:

" Ill-starred Nicanor, you were doomed to the foaming sea,
     Lying naked by now on some alien sandy shore,
 Or cast up remote on rocks, and all your happy home
     Is lost, and lost your hope of coming home to Tyre;
 Nothing of all your wealth could save you, O the pity!
     You're dead, and all your labours gone to the fishes and the sea."

Cargoes and lives were easily lost; and, if he kept his

life, many a Roman merchant must like Antonio have had reason to lament " my ships have all miscarried, my creditors grow cruel, my estate is very low, my bond is forfeit." On the other hand, if transport was limited and precarious, the Roman merchant was at an advantage on the monetary side. The Roman Empire was a great Free Trade whole; there were no protective tariffs, only very moderate customs-dues, and he enjoyed a banking and credit system, operating by means of bills of sale and bankers' drafts, almost as elaborate as our own.

Typical of the class is the upstart ex-slave Trimalchio —a character in the first Roman novel, the *Satyricon* of Petronius (written half-way through the first century A.D.):

" Yes, once I was like you, but thanks to my ability I've come to what you see. It's brains that makes the man; the rest's trash. I buy cheap and sell dear. Other people may have different ideas. I'm running over with good luck. As I was saying, it's my careful management that has brought me all this wealth. I was only as big as that lamp when I came from Asia; in fact I used to measure myself by it every day. By heaven's help I became master in the house and then I caught the fancy of my fool of a master. So when he died he made me and the Emperor joint-heirs, and I got a senator's fortune. But you've never got enough in this world. I wanted to go into business. To cut a long story short, I built five ships, loaded them all with wine—it was worth its weight in gold then—and sent them to Rome. Every blessed ship was wrecked as surely as if I'd ordered it; that's a fact. In one day Neptune swallowed up thirty million sesterces. Do you think I lost heart? Not a bit of it. The loss only whetted my appetite. It was as if nothing had happened. I built more ships, bigger, better and luckier ones, so that nobody could say I wasn't a man of courage. You know a great ship has strength in it. I loaded them with wine again, and this time I put in some pork, beans, perfumes and slaves as well. Then the wife did a decent thing. She sold all her jewelry and dresses and put 100 pieces of gold in my hand. This was like leaven to my fortune. What Heaven wants comes quickly. In one trip I cleared a cool 10,000,000. What did I do then? I bought back at once all the estates which had belonged to my master, I built a house and traded in cattle. Everything I touched grew like a honeycomb. When I found that I had more behind me than all the towns-folk put together, I quit the counter and set up my freedmen in business for me. Then I built this house. As you know, it was a regular bit of slum. Now it's fit for a god: four dining-rooms upstairs, my own bed-rooms, a couple of marble colonnades, my own private bedroom, the old vixen's sitting-room, not to mention a very fine porter's lodge and spare rooms for guests. Take my word for it. If you've only got a cent, you're valued at a cent. If you've got something, you'll be thought worth something. So your humble servant who used to be a pauper is now a prince."

" To India," says Horace, wishing to stress the fact that the merchant's calling takes him to the ends of the earth; and the mention of India is no eccentricity. For in the first century A.D. the commerce between Alex-andria and Italy was fed largely by the steadily growing trade with India. Once Hippalus had discovered the secret of the monsoons a direct commerce between India and the great Mediterranean emporia was possible. Chance has preserved for us, in the document called " Voyage round the Red Sea," a merchant's log which tells us some details of that commerce. The author of the log is nameless, but it is clear that he was an old sailor, possibly a Greek of Alexandria who had made the trading trip to India many times. We can see him starting his voyage from Egypt down the Red Sea in June in time to pick up the S.W. monsoons in July when he gets into the open sea in the south. He will have on board above all a good supply of Roman gold coin, for that commanded intense respect throughout the East; " the great thing about this Roman money," said a native ruler in Ceylon to a Roman visitor, " is that though the coins are struck by different kings and have different heads on them, they are all the same weight." This attitude was so much appreciated and exploited by Mediterranean merchants that the constant drain of bullion from West to East was one of the factors which in later days upset the economic stability of the Empire. Beside the coin the trader would take costly articles in gold and silver for wealthier customers and plenty of humbler commodities—cups, knives, beads, bright fabrics, various implements of iron, glass and the like. There would usually be a market for certain kinds of wine and jars of olive-oil.

Down the Red Sea our trader would sail, calling in at any likely port on the way. His log mentions these ports, noting the navigational dangers and giving tips about the sort of reception a trader might expect. His route lay through the straits of Bab-el-Mandeb, along the Somaliland coast to the " Cape of Spices " (Cape Guardafui). Once in the Indian Ocean, the monsoon brought him to India in forty days. He lists the Indian ports, the most important of which was Barygaza (the modern Broach), and warns captains of the difficulties created by the coastal tides in the business of putting in.

In the harbour he would discharge his cargo and load for the return journey with cotton and silks, spices and drugs and pepper (for which the Mediterranean world made ever-increasing demands). If he ventured farther south, he might lay in a supply of precious stones, diamonds, sapphires, pearls and ivory as well. In December the N.E. monsoon begins to blow, and that would be the time for setting on the homeward run. Navigational difficulties and a doubtful reception in unfamiliar ports made the whole thing a risky business, but once back in Egypt, if his luck held, he might reckon to make a 100 per cent. profit on most of his luxury freight. A dozen such journeys, and he might find himself well enough off to retire to a comfortable old age in his home town, a man of consequence and a pillar of local society.

THE LAWYER

The truth is that there were very few professions open to the gentleman in Rome. He could not, like his modern counterpart, go into business, for a direct part in commercial and industrial undertakings was forbidden to senatorial houses; he could not become a doctor or an accountant or a surveyor or an architect, for such things were left to Greeks, freedmen and slaves. There remained the Services, the Army and the imperial administrative service (for an able man the two were hardly separable in terms of a career), and the Law. Here was the one purely civil profession open to the gentleman. The amateur status of the lawyer may be gauged from the fact that in theory the pleader received no fee for his services (such was the ruling of a law passed in 204 B.C. and renewed by Augustus). Nevertheless, there can be no doubt that there was no lack of means for circumventing this embargo and receiving far higher fees than the very modest fees allowed by an enactment of Claudius, and that under the Empire a skilful speaker could make a fortune at the bar. The satirist Juvenal in the very poem in which he laments the painfully miscellaneous payments in kind for which a pleader might look for his services in court—a keg of sprats, a ham, flagons of questionable wine—comments on the smart dress and the flashing rings which a prospering barrister flaunts in court to advertise success and to attract business, much as a modern satirist might comment on the imposing motor-car in which a fashionable doctor goes his rounds.

We have seen in an earlier chapter something of the way in which Roman law grew up and of the way in which it worked. For better or worse, the law at Rome was largely in the hands of public men. Knowledge of the law was gained empirically, and its possessor was in theory bound to set his experience at the public service. It was left to the initiative of any citizen who felt himself so qualified to conduct an important criminal charge such as in any modern State would be brought by a public prosecutor. For the young man making a bid for position the undertaking of such a prosecution was a recognized expedient. It was thus that in the year 70 B.C. Cicero undertook the prosecution of Verres for misgovernment in his province of Sicily. The story is worth elaborating for the information it gives us on the legal career.

Verres had been governing Sicily for three years in a scandalous fashion, filling his own pockets and riding roughshod over justice. He was openly arrogant about

it, declaring that his spoils of the first year gave himself
a fortune, the spoils of the second would buy him the
best legal defence he could get, and that his third year
would pay for the bribing of the jury. The Sicilians
placed their case in the hands of Cicero, who had been
a quaestor in Sicily a short time before. But the nobles
who were then running the political racket decided that
in their interests Verres must be acquitted. Accordingly a counter-prosecutor, one Caecilius, was put up,
ostensibly hostile to Verres but in reality to engineer
his acquittal. Before the case could come on, the court
had first to decide which of the two claimants should
prosecute. The process of decision was called *divinatio*;
in this, as the extant speech shows, Cicero had little
difficulty in setting his claims above those of his rival
and in securing the decision. He was then granted a
period of a hundred and ten days in which to assemble
his evidence. Verres immediately made arrangements
for the prosecution of some unknown senator for misgovernment in Achaea, in which the prosecutor said that
he could have his case ready two days earlier. His
intention was that this faked case should take possession
of the one court in which such cases were tried and so
postpone his own trial perhaps until the year 70 was
over. Cicero defeated this scheme by the despatch with
which he marshalled his evidence; in fifty days he was
back in Rome. The trial began on August 5. But
there were still other factors to contend with. At the
beginning of the next year a number of the leading
magistrates due to take up office were friends of Verres,
among them three members of the powerful aristocratic
family the Metelli. There were many days of festival
ahead, on which legal business could not take place,

witnesses were being tampered with, and if the trial could be dragged out over the end of the year Verres would have strong hopes of an acquittal. In these circumstances Cicero altered the usual tactics. Instead of launching a long opening address, he decided to lay his main cards on the table without delay and to proceed as soon as possible with the examination of witnesses. After a brief introductory speech, the celebrated *in C. Verrem actio prima*, he warned the jury of the dangers afoot. The interrogation of witnesses took nine days; after three days the impression made by them was so unmistakable that Verres threw up the case, went into voluntary exile to Marseilles and was condemned in absence. The remaining five speeches which Cicero had ready, a full and eloquent exposition of Verres's crimes, were never delivered. They remain, even when allowance for exaggeration is made, a standing testimony to the abuses of which the republican system of provincial administration was capable in the hands of an unscrupulous clique; in oratory they are comparable with the denunciations of Warren Hastings by Burke and Sheridan.

The story of the trial of Verres suggests the many impediments against which the young lawyer must learn to contend in that age. A higher magistrate could forbid a magistrate of lower rank to proceed with a trial; there was a right of veto which could be exercised by a higher magistrate, or a magistrate of equal standing, against the execution of sentence; there were the tribunes of the people, who could interfere at any point, during a trial or after it, before the penalty was imposed.

Juries, the select citizen-panels on which the lawyer had to make his impression, varied greatly both in num-

ber and in composition. In the standing criminal
courts from 123 B.C. juries were drawn entirely from the
class of equites. This meant that juries were prejudiced
in the interests of the business men against senatorial
defendants, and Sulla, reforming the constitution in
conservative interests, transferred the right of sitting on
these juries from the equites to senators. By a law of
70 B.C. juries were shared between senators, equites and
a third obscure class denoted by the term " tribunes of
the treasury." Under Julius Caesar this third class
disappears ; Augustus reinstated it and shared juries
between its members and equites. A further provision
of the law of 70 was that juries should be drawn from
a standing list of 900 names, drawn up by the urban
praetor; but it seems that the court for extortion offences
alone had a list of 450.

The numbers of a jury in individual trials appear to
have varied for the most part between 50 and 75. Both
the defendant and the prosecutor had a say in its actual
constitution. The law of 122 B.C., which regulated trials
for extortion, provided that the prosecutor should select
100 names from the panel of 450, and that the defendant
should then reject fifty of these, leaving fifty to constitute
the operative jury. On occasion the procedure was
varied to minimize chances of bribery. The following
extract from a letter of Cicero, describing the trial of
Clodius in 61 B.C. (on a charge of violating the sanctity
of a women's festival), throws light on the atmosphere
in which this process might work:

> " The challenge took place amid general clamour,
> the prosecutor like an honest scrutinizer rejecting all
> the bad characters and the defendant like a well-
> meaning gladiator-manager removing all the respect-

PLATE XV.—ROMAN VILLA AT FOLKESTONE.

The aerial photograph brings out well the ground-plan of a corridor-type house with wings.   Above it on the left is the group of outbuildings.

PLATE XVI.—1. SACRIFICIAL RELIEF IN THE FORUM AT ROME.
A pig, sheep, and bull, a traditional offering in a public sacrifice (*suovetauralia*).
They are seen in a sacrificial procession.

2. THE APPIAN WAY, fringed with tombstones.

able persons; so that when the jury took their seats decent people began to feel many misgivings. You could not have found a more rascally crew in any underworld cabaret—senators of doubtful reputation, penniless knights, tribunes of the treasury, whose only claim to a title implying pay was their readiness to take it. Still there were a few honest men left whom he hadn't been able to get rid of, and there they sat in that alien company thoroughly miserable and painfully aware of their degrading fellows. . . . When I was brought up as a witness, the uproar from Clodius's supporters must have been loud enough for you to hear. . . ."

He goes on to describe the rest of this scandalous trial:

" You know our friend Calvus. . . . In two days, with one slave—an ex-gladiator at that—he had settled the whole business. He sent for the jury, promised, gave security, paid cash on the spot—and worse. . . . And yet, with all decent people leaving the scene, with the Forum full of slaves, there were twenty-five jurymen stout enough in the face of all that to prefer death to destroying all principle. There were thirty-one who were swayed more by hunger than by honour. Catulus met one of them and said ' Why did you ask for a bodyguard ? were you frightened of losing your money ? ' That, as briefly as I can tell, is the sort of trial it was and the reason for the acquittal."

The trial of Clodius was an extreme instance of jobbery, aggravated by political motives in the background, but it is an indication of what the lawyer might have to face. When we add that there was no machinery for excluding malicious allegation and irrelevancy either in pleading or in cross-examination, that abuse of the other side was a recognized device, that the appeal to emotion

9

was invariably stressed more than the appeal to reason (the accused invariably appeared unshaved and in mourning and made public parade of tearful relations), it will be seen that the lawyer's career was a more strenuous one in ancient Rome than it is in modern times.

Under the regimented government of the Principate the courts were quieter but in proportion to their quietness gave less scope for free speech and bold oratory to shine. Of the practice of law under the Emperors something has been said in a previous chapter. We will conclude with two passages from writers of imperial times. The first is from Tacitus's *Dialogue on Oratory*:

" Though our modern system is better adapted to our needs, yet the old courts were a better school for eloquence. There no one had to restrict his pleading to a limited time, nor was there any restriction on adjournments. Each speaker took as long as he liked and there was no limit to the duration of cases or to the number of counsel. . . . Much important business used to be tried before the praetor; cases which now come before the Hundred-board Court, now considered the most important, were so entirely overshadowed by other courts that there is no record of a speech by Cicero or Caesar or Brutus or Caelius or Calvus or of any great orator delivered before the Hundred-board. . . . In our day oratory suffers from the fact that almost all cases are heard in lecture-rooms and offices. It needs a broad track to test a good horse. So it is with speakers. . . . In our day careful speech-preparation is lost. The jury is always interrupting. You begin, have to answer a question and begin again. The judge is constantly stopping you for evidence to be taken and witnesses examined. And all the time there are only one or two people in

court to listen to you. . . . An orator needs appreciation and applause."

Such is the plea of a die-hard; but if the grand manner
had passed away with the old fire and faction, law was
more systematized and equitable in its working.   Still
there was room for careers; Quintilian, writing an educational treatise in the second half of the first century A.D.,
labels it *The Training of the Orator*, and his pupil,
the younger Pliny, has left us in his writings many
glimpses of an active court-life which he obviously
enjoyed.   Against the passage from Tacitus just quoted
we may set a few lines from one of Pliny's letters:

" The other day I had to speak in the Hundred-
board Court and found no way to my place except
through the tribunal and the jury!   Every other space
was packed.   And one young man who is quite a
figure in Rome got his tunic torn, as sometimes
happens in a crush, and stood there wrapped only in
his toga and for seven hours—that's the time my
speech took; a great effort, but it paid."

CRAFTS AND INDUSTRY

In early Rome there were few crafts.   Latium was a
land of farmers who could get a good livelihood from
their fields and had no need of seafaring.   Thus Rome
had no urge to compete with the industries and trade of
the commercial peoples about her, the Etruscans early
famous for their bronze-ware, pottery and terra-cottas,
the Greeks of Massilia (Marseilles) who brought metals
from the north, the Carthaginians already at home in
world-markets.   Under the Etruscan domination during the last century of the kingship, it is true, Rome was

lifted up to something approaching industrial eminence. In those days there were coppersmiths and goldsmiths, tanners and shoemakers, potters and dyers in Rome, even organized, said tradition, in guilds; and the ambitious buildings of the Tarquins brought in skilled artificers from Etruria and the Greek colonies of the south. Yet even so most of the craftsmen must have been foreigners imported by the alien dynasty, not Roman, and after the abolition of the monarchy there is little evidence of any but the humblest crafts working for home needs in republican Rome until Rome was well set on the path of world empire. Yet however small the bulk of Roman commerce, Roman traders there must have been from earliest times; we find evidence of them in the middle of the fourth century B.C., when a treaty with Carthage expressly excludes Roman traders from certain Carthaginian lands.

At no time can the free artisan have had a very happy lot in Rome. Slave labour was vastly cheaper, and its very existence made it impossible for workmen to use modern strike methods to improve their condition. If the free artificer put down his tools and refused to work, society could do without him and no object was served. Nor were the Senate interested in promoting industry; for senators were forbidden by law to engage in commerce. The capitalist class, the *equites*, found it expedient to employ slave labour usually on a large scale and tended to ignore free labour. There were no protective tariffs for home industry. Add to this the fact that manual labour and craft of any kind was considered servile and unworthy of a free man, and it will be seen that the citizen-artisan in Rome worked against great odds. Here is a passage from Cicero on the point:

" Which professions are to be held honourable ?
My opinion is this: any profession that incurs a general
distaste is to be condemned; for instance, those of the
tax-collector and the money-lender. Similarly the
profession of a worker for wages is a low calling . . .
his wage is nothing but the gratuity given to a slave.
The buying and selling of goods by retail is also de-
meaning; for your retailer can have no profit unless
he cheats, and nothing is more detestable than cheating. Every industrial worker follows a sordid calling.
. . . But the most to be deplored are the professions
that serve the pleasures of the sense: fishmongers,
poultry-sellers, cooks, purveyors of unguents, dancers
and jugglers. . . . The merchant who sells miscellaneous goods cannot be held respectable, but respect-
ability may be achieved by the wholesale dealer who
sells without cheating; and such a one who . . . is
satisfied with a moderate profit and returns from the
sea to settle on his estate even merits praise. But of
all occupations not based on speculation, the best,
most happy and most worthy is that one which is
open to all and designed for the free man—agriculture."

Whatever patrician opinion might be, there remained
classes which could not afford such a sense of *dignitas*.
Livings had to be earned, and within modest limits
there could not fail to be a ready market for the work
of the small proprietor-craftsman. To ignore the
existence of such is as bad as to suppose that the villas
figured in the text-books were the standard dwellings
of the population of Rome. In every town could be
found shoemakers, tanners, weavers, blacksmiths, carpenters, millers who were also bakers, fullers and
launderers and dyers, and small shop-keepers of all
kinds. Tanners and fullers needed a fairly elaborate
equipment and might run to fairly large establishments;

we can see the remains of these at Pompeii, Herculaneum and Ostia, and there is a good hint of the plant required for a dyeing business to be seen at the villa near Chedworth in Gloucestershire. Yet such industries remained on a small scale. In an age which knew little machinery more elaborate than the hand-loom and the hand-mill there were no factories comparable to those of modern times.

Particular towns might develop special manufactures: Capua became a noted centre for small metal-ware and household furniture, a number of towns such as Arretium in Etruria and Arelate in Gaul came to turn out pottery on mass-production lines; but, as the imperial prosperity developed, Italy came to import manufactured articles increasingly, and, in the absence of any protective legislation, the competition from the provinces slowly suppressed any economic vitality Italy might have had.

Artisans in the Roman world were regularly found organized in trade-guilds (*collegia*). Rich men's guilds did exist which were not merely parochial affairs, but most of these guilds were purely local organizations; the carpenters, the shoemakers, the cloth-workers in a town would be severally attached to the guilds of their calling. Unlike the guilds of medieval times, these organizations had no economic motive, as, for example, the maintaining of a monopoly or the regulation of apprenticeship and wages; they were much more like the provident societies than the trade-unions of our day. Membership was voluntary. The new member paid an entrance fee and small subscription and in return received the right to share in the meetings and religious rites of the club (each *collegium* had its patron god, and the religious element seems generally to have been well marked) and, in the case of illness or poverty, in any money-benefits that the club might provide. In some instances the only benefit provided appears to have been that of a burial-grant.

Under the Republic the trade-guilds might be used for political ends and their influence in this aspect was so dangerous that they were abolished by law in 64 B.C. They sprang up again, were repressed by Julius Caesar, and restored by Augustus in the quieter conditions of the Principate. They came to play an important part in social life in the Hellenized provinces of the East and were often used to promote social services such as those of fire-brigade and public transport. Even so the central authority at times viewed them with misgiving, as we can see from the correspondence between Trajan and the younger Pliny. In the third century the guilds became state-institutions and hardened, like the military *colonatus*, into something approaching feudal serfdom. Work became conscripted, hyper-organized, burdensome and hereditary. But in the great age of Rome they were still powers for the private good of their members, a minor illustration of the elastic corporateness which was the secret of Rome's success.

CHAPTER VII

THE GODS

Nam quantum ferro tantum pietate potentes
stamus.—Propertius.

" For we stand firm and strong as much in devoutness as in the sword."

" WE have overcome the nations," says Cicero, " because of our goodness and our heedfulness of the
divine and because of the special insight by which we
have come to see that the world is directed and governed
by the will of the Gods." *Dis te minorem quod geris
imperas*, Horace tells the Roman: " you rule the world
because you walk humbly before the Gods " (the phrase
is strongly reminiscent of the famous utterance of the
Hebrew prophet Micah), and in the forefront of the
Emperor's activity in the new age of peace are his
measures to restore to their full dignity the traditional
Roman religion and to reform society along religious
lines.

It is tempting to discount these claims as the products
of pietism and complacency, but, when we have made all
allowance for the element of exaggeration which must
inevitably be present in all propaganda, they remain
substantially true. The word *religio* which Cicero finds
a specially Roman characteristic means strictly a careful
attention to, a being bound by, the manifestations of the
divine. It is the positive word for which *negligo* (" I
neglect ") supplies the negative. Religion is in fact the
exact opposite of neglect. No people, as is abundantly
clear from the pages of their great historian Livy, can

have been more careful to note signs and portents and
prodigies from heaven; for these constituted, to those
who had ears to hear, the language in which the gods
spoke to men. The Roman word *fatum* (fate) means
originally " that which is spoken," that is the voice
which sets destiny on its course. Roman historians are
continually showing the march of portent and event in
the progress of history, the foreshadowing of events in
signs and wonders, the fulfilment of prophecies. That is
why their pages, even late in the Empire, are full of
prodigies; each one is a milestone on the march of Fate.
The wise look for these signs of the Divine Order,
observe them and shape their own actions accordingly;
the ungodly neglect them and are confounded.

Other peoples have conceived of history as a morality
play in which the sinful suffers and the righteous reaps
his due reward: when a people offends against the gods
it is punished, as Judah was punished by Sennacherib
and Nebuchadrezzar and as Persia was punished at
Salamis and Plataea; when it keeps the Word of God
it triumphs as the children of Israel at the River Kishon.
But the Roman, not being an intellectual like the Greek
or a creature of passion like the Jew, but a man of action,
was not sufficiently interested in other people's history
to conceive of History as Drama, and had too much
confidence in his own destiny to regard his own history
as other than a successful and ordered process. The
heart of the matter is that the Roman had a very
different conception of Time from that of the Greeks.
The Greeks lived in the present, content like children
with the sensation of the moment, and if ever they were
discontented with the present they turned their eyes to
the contemplation of a Golden Age in the remote past,

not to the future.[1] For the Greeks the divine was eternal,
outside the world of time. The Roman on the other
hand was acutely aware of the successive stages by which
past, present and future are related. A good illustration
of this difference is afforded in the syntax of the two
languages: Greek syntax, like English, is comparatively
easy-going about degrees of time, Latin is precise (" I'll
see you when I come," we say; ". . . when I *shall have
come*," says Latin). So it was with the Roman idea of
history and of the divine. For the Romans the gods
manifested themselves to men in time and were constantly so manifesting themselves. Hence the Roman
insistence on recording the precise moment of omens
and signs; such signs were to them connected in time
and marked a definite progression. To the casual eye
these little happenings—the way a bird flew past or the
noise it made, odd things in the behaviour or in the
bodies of animals—might seem trivial and unconnected,
but to the *religiosus* (" the god-conscious man ") they

[1] The same idea is found in certain Roman writers. But it is not
indigenous. It is a literary convention taken over from the Greeks.
Horace's well-known stanza:

> *damnosa quid non imminuit dies ?*
> *aetas parentum peior avis tulit*
> *nos nequiores, mox daturos*
> *progeniem vitiosiorem*

(" What is there that destructive Time has not impaired ? The generation of our fathers was worse than that of our grandsires and has begotten
us more worthless still, in our turn to produce a yet corrupter race ")

is far less typical of his outlook than that of the preceding poem in which
he sings that God's in his Heaven, all's right with the world and Augustus
marches on. We may recall, too, Lucretius's impressive exposition of
human evolution and think of Virgil's prophecy of a Golden Age in his
fourth Eclogue and of the progressive outlook of the early imperial age, as
well seen in coin-legends as in imperial pronouncements such as those of
Claudius.

made sense. History was not just chance. It had a
plot. It was in such apparently trivial happenings that
the gods were marking the path by which the Roman
State was to go in the march of time.

Scholars no longer talk of the birth of Roman religion
as a simple pure thing evolved by the earliest Romans
(though the later Romans liked to think that it was, as
they liked to think of the Roman character). The
Romans as we know them were a comparatively late
emergence and the result of many Italic, pre-Italic and
Greek influences. So, too, was their culture. The history of their religion is a long and tangled skein which is
only with great difficulty to be unravelled from a minute
and painstaking scrutiny of linguistic, archaeological
and later literary evidence, and as such cannot be considered here. But, however composite and derivative
the materials of Roman religion may have been, it is
undeniable that on the threshold of Roman history they
were moulded together into a form which can without
inaccuracy be labelled with the unique stamp of *Rome*.
Just as the Roman we know in history had a genius for
borrowing useful ideas from other people and combining
them with others to new practical purposes of his own,
so in the body of ritual which came to constitute the
" state religion " of Rome we recognize a formative
shape and an attitude which are not borrowed but
originally Roman. Unconscious borrowings and accretions are at first insensibly and then at a later stage (as in
the second phase of Hellenism when contact with Greek
culture was deliberately sought at the fountain-head)
deliberately reshaped.

It was in this later stage that the traditional religion
became self-conscious. As Rome's horizons widened in

the course of her territorial expansion, new influences came in from the East. As the simple agricultural community was superseded by City economics, there grew up the mob, a floating mass of humanity landless and irresponsible without roots in the soil. There came in new mystery religions, often in debased forms, which cut across the old traditions and beliefs, threatening not merely the old order of ideas but the old order of society. Against these dangerous forces the Roman aristocracy sought to bolster up the religion of their fathers by show-ing it as one with the Roman State. This was the age in which the conception of the Roman character, of the simple clear-cut trinity, *gravitas*, *simplicitas* and *pietas*, was formed and enunciated and projected into a distant past.[1] It needed only the emergence of an Augustus to crystallize this new version of the Roman culture and to give conservative propaganda the strength of tradi-tion. Thus the Augustan age is the classic age of Roman religion. In it the canons of religious observance were laid down once and for all and an official State religion came into being. There were of course accretions as time went on, but for the next two centuries the forms established in the Age of Augustus were rigidly retained.

What was the ancient religion of Rome ? Who were the old Roman gods ? We are apt to think of them as definite personalities with clear-cut shapes, because Roman deities came to be forced into Greek moulds almost as soon as the Romans became aware of Greek culture as something superior to their own. They identi-

---

[1] Here, again, the influence of Greek ideas is clearly marked. But, whereas the Greeks set the Golden Age in the *legendary* past, the Romans gave the idea a new force by associating it with the *historic* past.

fied their own gods with the great Greek gods, so that today we regard the names Jupiter and Zeus, Minerva and Athene, Juno and Hera as interchangeable. In fact the Roman terms tend to predominate; we speak of Venus when we mean Aphrodite, even of Mars when we mean Ares. For in spite of the centuries-old acceptance of these identifications they give a misleading picture of Roman religion. Jupiter was not Zeus, nor was Mars essentially a god of war. The crux of the difference between Greek and Roman religion is that the primitive Roman religion had no personal gods, only powers, unseen presences, vague brooding spirits acting on the life of man. These powers were called *numina*, and the word comes from *nuere*, " to nod," signifying will-power which might be exercised for human good or for human ill. Religion was the calculated attempt to bring it about that these powers, named but not known, were directed to the good of man.

The family was the stronghold of religion, and it is in the home that we find the oldest gods: *Vesta* the goddess of the hearth, cherishing the fire which is the token of family community; *Janus* the door-god who is the spirit of the door which guards the family from the outside world; the *Penates*, the guardians of the family larder; the *Lares* who watch over the fields which give the food; the *genius*, the life-spirit of the family continuing from generation to generation. To all these spirits simple offerings would be made at special places and times. For every phase of human activity had its godward side. Out-of-doors there were two great powers, Mars and Jupiter, and a multitude of others. Mars was originally, it seems, a spirit of the wild, a power which the farmer had to propitiate to keep ruin from his land and its crops.

Later, when the farmer went forth into unknown land to fight for Rome, there too he felt himself going into the province of Mars, and Mars became at least in part a god of war. The impact of the Greek war-god Ares caused the primary nature of Mars to be forgotten. Jupiter was the great sky-spirit which sends the rain and the lightning and the thunder, to bless or to smite the works of men. Very early in the life of Rome he became the greatest god, the father-spirit of Rome and was given a temple on the Capitol, the heart of Rome. With him went Juno, the deity who watched over matrons and their lives, and Minerva, the patroness of craftsmen.

From the religion of the home developed that of the State. Rome, too, had her hearth watched over by Vesta and the virgin-priestesses, the Vestal virgins, who tended her sacred flame. Janus, too, came to receive a shrine from the State, from which he presided over the opening of the State-door which is the New Year. As Rome encountered other peoples and their ways, other gods were introduced: Hercules, and Castor and Pollux (who came from Greek sources), and some from near at hand as Diana, a local wood-spirit who rose to inherit all the prestige of Artemis and Hecate.

We may speak of the State religion, for the State came to have its fixed Calendar with its list of deities and days and code of ritual directions on the choice of sacrificial victims and the formulae to be used in offering them. But only an antiquarian would know them all; they were so numerous and there was so much overlapping. And it is difficult for us to appreciate a religion which had no theology, which prescribed no creed and carried no essential moral content, a religion which was in fact more a body of usages stiffening into ritual than a rule for life.

We note, too, the absence of any such centralized organization or control as we are accustomed to in the modern world. The State was, it is true, aware of the need to do all it could to secure the goodwill of the *numina* for the corporate welfare of Rome: it gave careful directions for ritual worship; but there was no central provision for the training of a priestly order; there was no exclusive priestly profession; the same man might be the holder of a public office and a member of a priestly board. In the early days when Rome was ruled by kings, the king was the religious head of the State, supported by an advisory body of *pontifices* (" pontiffs "). When the monarchy was abolished, this body under the chief pontiff (*pontifex maximus*) became the supreme religious authority (the title is still held by the Pope). The pontiffs (fifteen in number by the end of republican times) were chiefly concerned with the legal aspects of religion, ritual being under the control of the *Rex sacrorum*, an official appointed for life by the chief pontiff. Other priestly boards controlled particular aspects of religious function: the *augures* were devoted to the interpretation of the omens obtained from the flight and behaviour of birds and of other celestial portents such as those contained in lightning and thunder: the *haruspices* were charged with the art of divination based on the inspection of the organs of the sacrificed beasts; the *fetiales* directed the ritual associated with the making of war and peace. Among other such colleges the Salii (" the dancing priests ") conducted the ritual worship of Mars, the Arval brethren controlled the propitiation of the powers which gave fertility to the ground.

Vesta, the goddess of home and hearth, had her six nun-like priestesses who cherished the sacred flame in the Temple of Vesta, the hearth of the Roman State. A Board of Ten, *decemviri sacris faciundis* (in the time of Augustus they had become fifteen), had charge of the Sibylline books, ancient mysterious prophetic records which legend said had been bought from the Sibyl of Cumae by one of the Tarquin kings. These books contained certain directions for religious procedure, in accordance with which certain spectacular rites of a public nature were introduced: the *supplicatio*, in which the people decked themselves in festal array and carried laurel boughs in procession to certain temples in thanksgiving for some great event; the *lectisternium* (or Spreading of Couches), at which images of the gods were set on couches with food offerings in front of them and so borne in public; the *ludi*, great athletic contests and dramatic festivals to the honour of various deities.

All these ceremonies were Greek in origin and their introduction one of the many instances of the Hellenization of Roman religion. Cumae was an old Greek colony, and it was from Cumae that Apollo had been brought to Rome; he was given a temple there in the fifth century B.C. and came in time to rank as the equal of Jupiter himself.

In the great wars of the third century this religion, such as it was, came to undergo the severest of tests. Particularly in the long dragging Second Punic War, with Hannibal at large in Italy and disaster upon disaster, the morale of the nation came near breaking-point, and the authorities tried hard to bolster it up with elaborate religious rites of the type we have described. In the hour of calamity men fly to the gods, but the gods

PLATE XVII.—PUBLIC BUILDINGS IN ROME.

1. The Theatre of Marcellus: a good example of Roman arcading with the Greek orders (Doric, Ionic, and Corinthian, alternating as in the Colosseum) superimposed (see p. 209).

2. The Baths of Caracalla: ruins of the gigantic structure built at the beginning of the third century A.D., showing the Roman mastery of the arch on a large scale.

PLATE XVIII.—THE ARCH OF TITUS AT ROME.

Built in Pentelic marble and completed in A.D. 81 in commemoration of the
capture of Jerusalem.

in this case seemed sadly inadequate, and in the upshot the old religion was so shaken that it never regained its old strength. The most eloquent testimony to this failure is the desperate innovations to which the State resorted at certain crises. After the terrible defeat at Cannae the Romans even had recourse to human sacrifice; and in 205 B.C., when all hope of getting rid of the Carthaginians seemed gone, the Senate passed a decree authorizing the importation of the Eastern earth-goddess, Cybele, from Asia Minor, in the form of a shapeless black meteoric stone. The next year the stone was escorted in solemn procession and installed with a new wild order of festival of the most un-Roman kind in the temple of Victoria on the Palatine, where by 191 as the Great Mother, *Magna Mater*, it had a temple of its own.

Similarly un-Roman were the rites of Bacchus (Dionysus), which became popular in the first quarter of the next century and occasioned so much licence and scandal that the Senate issued a decree enacting severe measures to suppress them, declaring them a menace to the Roman State. Yet in a modified form the worship remained, as did other Oriental mystery-religions. For they provided an emotional outlet which the old religion did not give. In these cults the individual could feel a personal contact with the divine, could feel that in his worship his own life and salvation were at stake, could surrender himself with abandon to the inspiration and service of the god and feel himself at one with the earth, the wild and all the elemental forces of being. The rites of the earth-goddess Cybele, for instance, came to include a baptism in the blood of a bull which was the token of spiritual rebirth and the hope of redemption from sin and of a life hereafter.

10

While some orders of Roman society were attracted to these mystery-religions, individuals here and there, especially among the educated, found their spiritual needs better provided for in the teachings of Greek philosophy. Two schools of thought were especially prominent, Stoicism and Epicureanism. The followers of Epicurus preached a materialistic explanation of the Universe. Everything is composed of atoms, minute and indestructible material bodies in constant .motion, sometimes combining in momentary unions, sometimes dispersing, always in flux. The soul, too, is such a temporary union of atoms and is dissolved at death. There are no gods, for all is governed by immutable law; if there are gods, they have no interest or power in the affairs of men. There is no immortality. Men should make the most of the short life they have, living pleasurably and without illusions of a life beyond the grave. There is no Paradise for the good; neither is there any Hell. It is easy to see how such a philosophy has given us the word " epicure." But when the philosopher spoke of living pleasurably he thought not of eating and drinking and the other pleasures of the flesh, but of the refined pleasures of friendship and of the mind. His watchword was Tranquillity and his rule of life a detached but open-eyed awareness.

This philosophy was raised to sublime expression in the poem, " On the Nature of Things," by Lucretius, a poet of the age of Cicero. The poem is an inspired paradox. He writes to free men from the fetters of superstition, to proclaim that there are no gods, that the Universe is an intelligible, mechanical whole, composed of ever-moving atoms; that even the " soul " is only the result of a temporary combination of atoms and dis-

appears when that combination is dissolved. There is
then no immortality, no existence after death and therefore nothing to be feared. The odd thing is that he
preaches this doctrine with all the fervour of a religious
enthusiast; that it is for him a gospel of salvation. " O
death, where is thy sting ? O grave, where is thy victory ? "—the message, so absolute, so categorical, cannot
fail to be emotionally tinged, and it is only with difficulty
that in the homage he pays to the power of Nature and
in the invocation to Venus, the giver of life, we recognize
the voice of an atheist. But, however paradoxical the
content of the poem, there is no mistaking the honesty
and courage of its author, as his bold mind penetrates
the darkest problems of life, delighting in the complexity
and yet awed by the vastness, but above all resolved to
bring light to them that walk in darkness. He is a
master-spirit, scientist, philosopher and teacher; and
yet when all is said the last word must be that he was a
poet. That will do much to explain the mystery.

The philosophy to which Lucretius bore so eloquent
a witness must have attracted many followers among the
young intellectuals of late republican Rome (the poet
Virgil was for many years under its sway); but it was
too bloodless and resigned a creed to establish itself in
Rome. What Roman who was not poet enough to
discharge all his energies in the exercise of the mind
could find satisfaction in a teaching which reduced him
to the role of a spectator of life ? And if Epicureanism
was unsatisfactory for individual needs, how much less
satisfactory was it in its social aspects ? For, as Cicero
rightly urges at the outset of his treatise " On the Nature
of the Gods," if the atheists are right in saying that there
are no gods to interest themselves in the affairs of men,

where do right-doing and reverence and conscience find a place ?

Stoicism also preached a materialistic explanation of the Universe. But, where Epicureanism was negative in its import, Stoicism had a positive moral content. In other words, it was a religion, not a substitute for one. For it was a Greek scientific explanation of the Universe, animated by a belief in its ultimate goodness which was derived from Zoroastrianism, an ancient Persian religion which centred round a single god (whose symbol was fire) who warred against evil. This god served the same function as the Logos, the innate Word or Reason, which was in the beginning and was the controlling force of life. With this controlling spirit all good men could live in harmony, by living an austere, self-disciplined life. This was the aspect of Stoicism which caught the Roman mind. Its severe moral standards and its teaching that the good man should train himself to be independent of the world of flesh, that goodness is its own reward, secured a wide following throughout the Roman world of the early Empire and inspired some of its leading minds. Its working on a sensitive mind can be admirably gauged from the *Meditations* of the Emperor Marcus Aurelius, a Stoic who through a reign troubled by many struggles and misfortunes drew continual strength from meditation on the principles of his philosophy and their application to his own life. Under the Empire Stoicism flourished and was approved by the State, for it stood for the idea of corporate order and, in a fashion, inculcated a belief in monarchy.

It was as philosophy rather than as religion that Stoicism came to Rome and, as such, like Epicureanism it remained an affair for the individual, without social significance. When Augustus gave peace to the world and became its master, he saw the crying need for the unity of faith which a central religion with corporate expression can give. Accordingly he instituted a great revival of the old gods, of Mars, Apollo, Jupiter, of all the apparatus of the religion of Numa. To some extent he succeeded; the old religion came once more into the forefront of public consciousness, and the old rites were punctiliously enacted; but, beneath it all, the newer mystery-religions steadily gained ground.

Before we consider these mystery-religions, mention must be made of one last attempt to provide a religion which might hold good throughout the Empire. This was the worship of the Emperor. Julius Caesar was worshipped as a god after his death; so was Augustus, and in some parts of the Empire even in his lifetime, and, though the early Emperors deprecated the worship of themselves, the practice gradually extended until by the end of the first century A.D. an Emperor can begin an edict (referring to himself) with the formula *dominus ac deus noster* . . . The idea of deifying human beings after death was no new departure in Roman religion. For centuries men had prayed to the *di manes*, the Blessed Company of the Departed; Theseus, Latinus, Semo Sancus and Romulus had all been deified. As for the worship of the living, that admittedly was not Roman, but there was abundant precedent for that in the Hellenic East (Alexander had been worshipped, and the Ptolemies in Egypt and the Seleucids in Syria were regularly worshipped as gods while they were feared as kings), and the Hellenic East was now largely in the Roman Empire. Accordingly, when the Roman Emperor found provincial subjects anxious to accord to him in virtue of his position the homage which they had regularly paid to kings, he did not discountenance a practice which could be so valuable a bond of Empire.   So Emperor-worship came to have a long and complex history.   But, however grateful the subjects of the Empire were for the imperial achievement and the imperial peace, Emperor-worship was only a perfunctory expression of loyalty, in essence little more than saluting the Union Jack.   It could not be confused with the satisfaction of spiritual needs of men and women.   Even when set against Christianity, Emperor-worship was not a rival, but only a police-test for loyal subjects.   The Christian who refused to drop a pinch of incense into the flame in front of the Emperor's statue was regarded not so much as a heretic as a potentially disloyal subject.

From this brief Empire Day interlude we can return to the mystery-religions.   Two such cults, in particular, which gained great vogue in the early Empire, were those of Isis and Mithras.   Isis came from Egypt via the Hellenized Alexandria.   Her cult was domiciled in Italy during the last century B.C. and not wholly approved by the State.   There were a number of attempts to suppress this cult, and the Emperor Tiberius was moved by a certain incidental scandal connected with it to destroy her temple and prohibit her worship. But it went on.   Isis was the all-powerful queen of heaven and earth, of life and death, a gentle and mild deity, whose worship was made up mostly of morning and evening prayers, with hymns and litanies intoned by tonsured priests clad in white.   It carried a great appeal to the emotion and the imagination in its yearly Passion festival for the death of the god Osiris, the consort of Isis; and a great appeal to those with a

taste for the ascetic in the penances for sin which it provided. Mithras was an ancient Persian god brought
from the East by soldiers who had served there. He
stood as the champion of Light against the powers of
darkness. According to legend he had done a great
deed by the slaying of a bull (as St. George by the slaying
of the Dragon) and the deed was commemorated in a
ritual bull-slaying, shown in many ancient bas-reliefs,
which carried with it for the worshipper a baptism in
blood borrowed from the worship of Cybele. It was a
masculine religion, in which the initiate had to go
through several stages or degrees, and requiring a certain courage; as such it became above all the soldier's
religion.

Such religions, it will be seen, satisfied individual
yearnings not envisaged in the old order. That is the
secret of their persistence. But the final triumph was
to rest with another religion which, like Mithraism and
the cult of Isis, came out of the East and promised re-
generation. The gospel of Christ spread with phenomenal speed through the eastern half of the Empire,
and by the middle of the first century A.D. had en-
trenched itself in Rome. It attracted the lower classes
first and in spite of persecution worked its way steadily
ahead with its new and noble ethic through the upper
reaches of society until, by A.D. 313, the Emperor Constantine had proclaimed it the religion of the Empire.
Even after this date the old religion still lingered here
and there, the old rites maintained by die-hard families
even after the temples and priesthoods had been officially
abolished; but in the end they died, though some of the
old superstitions and usages survived, as we shall see,
within the Christian sphere.

As for the old pagan beliefs, the beliefs which Augustus sought to reinstate in the core of his new Roman State, let us not misunderstand them.   Time found them out, and they died because in the last resort they proved false, their magic idle, their mythologies an unavailing dream, their ethic negative and their theology a muddle.   Yet they had served as a nucleus and a symbol of the old corporate tradition, of individuals thinking not of themselves but gravely banded to serve the State amid the stresses imposed on things temporal by higher and dimly-apprehended powers.   Man lived and fought and died and went into the darkness to join the community of his fathers.   There were the death-masks of his ancestors to remind him of that fact.   The poets underlined it: *omnes eodem cogimur* (" we must all travel in that one direction ") sang Horace; " suns may set and rise again, but we, when once our little light is set, must sleep one everlasting night," says Catullus, in three exquisitely-chiselled lines:

> *soles occidere et redire possunt ;*
> *nobis, cum semel occidit brevis lux,*
> *nox est perpetua una dormienda.*

But the one direction, the one place, the one night was there.   It was in her unity that Rome was strong; and even in death the Roman was not alone.

Let us glance at the Roman religious festivals as they affected the lives of the citizens.   The whole year was carefully marked out in festivals month by month.   We can do no more than select a few.

Prominent among the Roman festivals we find those we expect to find in an agricultural community, those concerned with the beginning and end of the farmer's round, the praying for the increase of flocks and seed in spring and for a good harvest in late summer and autumn. In April, for instance, there was, on the 15th, the *Fordicidia*, at which pregnant cows and their unborn calves were sacrificed to the earth-goddess (Tellus, the same power represented in other aspects as Ceres) and burnt to ensure the increase of the corn now growing in the womb of earth; on the 19th the *Cerealia*, at which mysterious rites involving the loosing of foxes with burning torches fastened to their tails were enacted in worship of Ceres, the goddess of the fruits of earth. On the 21st the *Parilia*, when the farmer hung the sheep-fold with greenery and purified it with sprinkling and sweeping and made a great fire of olive-branches and bay, through which the shepherds leapt and the flocks were driven, and offerings of cake and milk were made to the pasture-god Pales; on the 25th came the *Robigalia*, when sacrifices were made to avert the red rust or mildew which attacks the corn in the ear. In May, on the 29th at the *Ambarvalia* (" The Festival of the Fields-Procession "), the farmer and his household went in solemn procession round the fields taking with them a bull, a sheep and a pig as sacrificial victims. Three times the company went round the land, and at the end of the third round the beasts were offered up to the accompaniment of a prayer to Mars (who was originally a farmers' god), asking for increase for the crops and herds and health for the household. The ritual prayer has been preserved in the writings of Cato and there is a beautiful allusion to the rite in Virgil's *Georgics :*

Thrice round the springing grain let go the auspicious beast,
With the accompanying train all jubilant,
Crying to Ceres to enter in their home. . . .

The *Ambarvalia* belonged to the time when the corn was first springing; in August came the festivals connected with harvest. On the 19th the *Vinalia*, when prayers were offered for the safe vintage of the all but matured grape, and on the 21st the *Consualia*, the festival of the storing of the harvest (Consus was the god of storage), when horses and asses had holiday and were garlanded with flowers, much as our horses are decked on May-day.

In December came the *Saturnalia*, the Roman equivalent of Christmas and in many ways the ancestor of our modern Christmas celebrations. The *Saturnalia* began on December 17th and lasted for several days (a practice echoed in our traditional song about the twelve days of Christmas). It began with a public sacrifice at the temple of Saturn (an old agricultural god identified with an ancient king of Latium in the old Golden Age), and this solemn ceremony was followed by a public feast at which there was general relaxation and senators and knights laid aside the toga. At the end of the feast the people dispersed to their homes with cries of "*Io Saturnalia!*" The next two days were universal holiday. On the 18th the day began in the home with the sacrifice of a sucking pig on the family hearth; presents were exchanged inside the family and between friends; there were callings from house to house, games, liberal eating and drinking and general merrymaking. Slaves were allowed to mix with their masters as though they were equals; sometimes slaves and masters changed places and masters waited on slaves. It was the season of peace and good-will among men, and people went about wishing each other *bona Saturnalia*. An interesting form of present commonly exchanged at this time was that of wax candles, thought to represent the increasing strength of the sunlight after the winter solstice, which falls about this time. The same idea is attached to our burning of the Yule log; and when guests and staff change places for an hour or so at the New Year in modern hotels, when we give our friends presents at Christmas, play games, partake of the family turkey and otherwise eat and drink more than we normally do and go about wishing each other a merry Christmas, we do these things largely because the Romans did them before us.

Modern affinities, though not so strikingly marked, are also to be found in the mysterious festival of the *Lupercalia*, which took place in February on the 15th. The festival began at a cave called the Lupercal at the foot of the south-west corner of the Palatine Hill with the sacrifice of a goat and a dog, rare and especially holy victims. Two noble youths then had their foreheads smeared with blood from the sacrificial knife, and the blood was then wiped away with wool dipped in milk. When this was done they were required to laugh. They then girded the skins of the slain beasts round their naked bodies, took strips of the same skins in their hands and at the head of two bands of young men ran round the base of the Palatine Hill, striking with the strips of skin at all women who met them. There has been much controversy on the meaning of this rite, but the main intentions seem clear. The first part of it is a ritual drama of the death and rebirth of the Vegetation-god who died every autumn and is born again every spring. By being smeared with the blood of the sacrificed animal the young men partake of the death of the Vegetation-god; by being wiped with milk-wet wool they partake in his re-birth (for milk is the first nourishment and symbol of life). " The laughing," as Warde Fowler says, " is the outward sign of such revival; for the dead are silent, they cannot laugh." Putting on the skins is a further entering into the reborn life of the dead spirit. The beating of others with strips of the same skin is to impart to them a share in the same regiving of life. That is why women, and especially barren women, stood in the path of the young men to be touched by the life-giving skin, that through its virtue they might conceive new life within them and give birth to children. Lastly, the running round the Palatine was a purificatory rite intended to lustrate the region, here symbolic of Rome, round whose boundaries they ran. It is here that the modern affinity appears, for in this last point the rite is one with the beating of bounds in solemn procession with peeled wands still observed in certain English parishes today. The ceremony, primitive and medicine-man-like though it seems, must have touched certain mainsprings of Roman religious feeling, for Augustus took pains to establish the festival as an essential item in the Roman year, and we are told that it was celebrated in Rome down to A.D. 494, when Pope Gelasius I did away with it and set in its place on the same day the Feast of the Purification of the Virgin Mary.

Another ceremony connected with boundaries, but of a simpler and different kind, was that of the *Terminalia* observed on the 23rd of February. The ritual, as Ovid describes it, is one which seems peculiarly appropriate to a people who were originally a simple farmer community and to a people with a strong sense of law and order. It was celebrated at places where the lands of two farmers were divided by a common boundary.

From each side comes the farmer with his dependants clothed in white, his wife bearing fire from the family hearth, his children bringing fruits and cakes for sacrifice. Each farmer garlands his side of the boundary stone they share. An altar is made, the fire kindled and the fruits of earth burned in the flames. A lamb and a ·sucking-pig are sacrificed and the boundary-stone sprinkled with their blood, and the ritual ends with a feast and hymns in honour of Terminus, the god of boundaries.

The mention of Terminus will serve to remind us of a striking characteristic of Roman religion: the multiplicity of its primitive gods and the fact that they are strictly departmental. Just as the boundary (*terminus*) had its own special spirit, so there was an attendant spirit for almost every phase of human activity. When the Roman was born into the world certain birth-deities delivered him, but Vagitanus ordered his first infant wail (*vagitus*), Cunina watched over him in his cradle (*cunae*), to be superseded by Cuba when he was big enough to sleep in a bed (*cubile*). Edusa presided over his first attempts to eat (*edere*), Potina over his first attempts to drink (*potare*). Statilinus taught him how to stand, and there were separate deities Abeona and Adeona to watch over his first infant ventures to and from the house. These are but a few from a long array of powers. So, too, the countryman had separate spirits of the hoe, of the plough, of reaping and garnering. Everywhere there were gods, spirits—they were not gods conceived in definite shape (sometimes their worshippers were not quite sure of their gender)—working in their special spheres, each controlling some aspect of human life. The same departmental conception of the divine powers survives in the worship of the Saints in the Latin Catholic countries to this day. The peasant in the south of Italy prays, for instance, to San Roque for protection against plague, but to Santa Lucia for deliverance from ophthalmia; in Spain one prays to San Francisco for colic, but to Santa Dorothea for rheumatism and so on. When the Roman in the course of his political and cultural expansion became aware of the Greek polytheism and came to adopt the Olympic gods, these were rather grafted on to the body of his religion than allowed to supersede the old order. But it was inevitable that Greek deities, fully-fledged in human form, with cult-statues and temples, with long legend and family relationships to lend colour and romance to their worship, should in many instances make the greater appeal. Many of the old Roman deities were saved by being identified with Greek (the Roman saw that Semo Sancus *was* Heracles, that Ceres *was* Demeter), but many of them must gradually have lapsed into oblivion.

With the multiplicity of deities and the absence of spiritual demands on the worshipper went tolerance. New deities might be approved and come to be accepted. What was not tolerated was intolerance, for intolerance implied an attack on the entire Roman system. The Christians in the early Empire were objected to because they would not live and let live; not content with worshipping their own God, they must needs condemn all others. In resisting such attacks conservatism was asserting not so much the State religion as the State of which it was the expression, the State which was willing to countenance and adopt anything which would conform to the Roman mould.

CHAPTER VIII

HOLIDAYS AND ENTERTAINMENTS

Idem populus . . . qui dabat olim
imperium, fasces, legiones, omnia, nunc se
continet atque duas tantum res anxius optat,
panem et circenses.—JUVENAL.

" The nation which once dispensed commands, rods of office, legions, everything—now keeps humbler aims and prays in all earnestness for two things only—bread and shows."

THE whole year, as we have seen, was marked out by regularly-spaced festivals in Rome.   So far we have considered mainly their religious aspect, but there were certain festivals which were observed with secular entertainments of an elaborate order.   Chief among these festivals were the games in honour of the earth-goddess Cybele, the *Megalensia,* celebrated in April; the *ludi Apollinares,* which fell in July, in honour of Apollo; the *ludi Romani* at the festival of Jupiter in September; and the *ludi plebeii* in November.   These festivals and others would be marked by great gladiatorial shows, wild-beast spectacles, races and plays.   Under the Republic it became increasingly common for the pre-siding magistrate to spend large sums of money on mak-ing the entertainment as spectacular as possible.   In this way men would remember his period of office, and the popularity gained would be valuable when he stood for higher office or needed public support for any scheme he or his party might have on hand.   For this reason, among others, shows multiplied steadily, political mag-nates vying to outdo each other in their bids for popular favour, until the satirists could gauge the degeneracy of the Roman commons by their addiction to the circus and amphitheatre. *Panem et circenses*; corn-doles and free shows were the sheet-anchors of proletarian content.

THE CIRCUS

Chariot-racing seems to have been popular from the earliest times, long before race-courses were known.   In imperial times Rome could boast three great race-courses: the Circus Maximus, which with successive enlargements grew from a modest ring of wooden seats into a magnificent construction, with an exterior of marble and an interior capable of seating some 150,000 spectators at a time; the Circus of Flaminius near the Campus Martius; and the Circus of Caligula, where Nero held his monstrous chariot-races by the light of burning Christians.   There were two more in the out-skirts of Rome on the Appian Way and another down the Tiber at the Sanctuary of the Arval Brethren.   The sport became no less popular in Italy generally and in the provinces, and many towns came to possess race-courses.   We find them in Gaul and Spain, in Africa and in the provinces of the East.

Early in its history chariot-racing came into the hands of professionals.   Companies financed by capitalists maintained stables and jockeys.   Each company or faction had its distinctive colour worn by its jockeys and in its horse-trappings.   The leading factions of early imperial times were the " reds " (*russata*), the " greens " (*prasina*), the " blues " (*veneta*) and the " whites " (*albata*).   These factions would enjoy varying periods of eminence, and their fortunes were followed with as much partisan enthusiasm as are professional League

PLATE XIX.—PUBLIC BUILDINGS IN A PROVINCIAL TOWN.

Arles in Roman France (see p. 234): the theatre is seen in the left foreground.

PLATE XX.—A ROMAN PROVINCIAL CITY.

The Forum at Timgad in Roman Africa.

football teams today. In interest the races offered the public the combined excitements of league football and horse-racing, but with a grimmer edge. Sharp practice among jockeys was common and encouraged, and a spill which involved bloodshed added zest for a Roman crowd which on other days of festival would take delight in watching armed men fight to the death. In the clash of interests in that crowd we should miss the sportsmanship and find the appraisal of skill overlaid in the violent frenzies of money-lust, blood-lust and mob-rivalries. Idolatry of successful horses and favourite jockeys was the natural consequence of a sport in which emotions ran high and undisciplined; and it is not surprising that some jockeys attained the celebrity and salaries of film-stars. Horse-racing maintained its popularity steadily under the later Empire, and in the Eastern Empire at Constantinople the party-faction of the colours ran so high that it often led to extensive rioting and political turbulence. It was here, incidentally, that the term " hippodrome," the Greek for " race-course," first came to prominence; its ubiquity in modern times as a name for theatres, music-halls and cinemas is a testimony to the domination exercised by horse-racing over ancient ideas of entertainment.

The course was oval in shape. Down the middle was built a thin central barrier or wall (*spina*) round which the teams had to race. Races were run anti-clockwise, and seven laps were usual. The starting-device consisted of a line of specially-constructed stalls with double doors. At the given signal, when the presiding magistrate dropped a white cloth from his box, the doors were thrown open and the teams shot out. The finishing-point was marked by a white line on the sand. Chariots

11

were frail and light and easily overturned, and drawn by four horses specially bred and trained for the purpose in Africa, it might be, or in Spain or Cappadocia or Thessaly.   Spills were common, and for protection the driver wore leggings and leather thongs wrapped round his body; he carried a whip (which he would not scruple to use on his opponents) and, tucked into a belt, a knife with which he cut himself free from the reins if he were upset.   For he drove with his reins wrapped round his body, to enable him to exert the greater power in manipulating them at the turns.   A skilled driver would almost graze his left wheel against the column of the *spina* at the turn, and many times he would have to swerve violently and suddenly to avoid a chariot which had come to grief in front of him.   The actual manipulation of the reins called for great skill, as two of his horses only were harnessed to the yoke on the chariot-pole; the two extreme outside horses were " tracers " harnessed by traces direct from the axle.

Other entertainments, too, could be seen in the circus. There were other exhibitions of horsemanship besides that shown in chariot-racing.   Sometimes there were equestrian performances similar to those which we can see at Olympia or in the Rushmoor arena today, horses doing elaborate tricks, dare-devil riding, cavalry man-oeuvres, and there was one ceremonial particularly worthy of note in which boys of aristocratic houses engaged on horseback in a complicated series of maze-like evolutions of traditional pattern, which included a mimic battle.   This exercise was supposed to be of great antiquity, even to derive from the Trojans whom legend claimed as the founders of Rome, and was in conse-quence called the Trojan Play (*lusus Troiae*).   However respected such a ceremonial might be, more popularity attached to the wild-beast fights and hunts which were commonly staged in the circus. Magistrates would go to great expense to provide animals of unusual type or in unusual quantities for this purpose. Lions, tigers, leopards and bears and other animals were imported in large numbers to be pitted against men, who were sometimes trained fighters, sometimes half-armed criminals and slaves.

Governors in eastern provinces were frequently pestered by their magistrate friends at home to send them panthers and leopards for their shows, as was Cicero in Cilicia by his friend Caelius. Entertainment so crude, in which wholesale carnage was more conspicuous than any display of courage or skill, would have been revolting to a modern spectator and serves even more effectively than gladiatorial contests to point the difference between modern and ancient tastes. Yet it is gratifying to note that even in the ancient world there were many minds which turned in loathing from such practices, and that even the mob on occasion cried out against mere butchery, as when Pompey offered up for its delectation a score of tame and bewildered elephants. Nor did such performances ever lose their ritual side. They always began with a stately procession behind the presiding magistrate, the performers, priests and ministrants all in due order with the apparatus of sacrifice and the images of gods and the effigies of deceased Emperors borne on high. Down from the Capitol through the Forum and so into the Circus the procession would wend its pompous way and right round the inside of the arena, and the performance could not begin until sacrifice had been publicly offered and found propitious.

THE AMPHITHEATRE

The circus was an elongated structure primarily intended to provide a race-course, the amphitheatre was designed for the benefit of spectators; a place, as the name says, where you could see all round (the theatre was more or less a half-circle with the round cut short by the stage; the amphitheatre was a complete round enclosing a circular arena in which men could fight). For that was its purpose, to house gladiatorial combats. This highly popular form of entertainment, though it did not take a general hold on Rome till the end of the second century B.C., derived from the Etruscan practice of sacrificing slaves and prisoners at the funeral of a great man. (It will be remembered that Achilles in the *Iliad* sacrifices twelve Trojans at the funeral of Patroclus, and that in the Funeral Games that followed ,was included an armed fight between Ajax and Odysseus.) The first amphitheatres were built in Italy in the middle of the first century B.C.; under the Empire many a provincial town could boast a fine amphitheatre of stone. Many of their remains can be seen today—at Verona (where the arena is still used for entertainments), at Pompeii, at Syracuse, at Arles and at Nîmes, at Corinth, at Merida in Spain, to name but a few. The most famous of all is that erected at Rome under Vespasian and Titus, the great Colosseum, a monumental structure with its triple arcading of Doric, Ionic and Corinthian pillars, still a massive landmark in Rome today and the titular progenitor of all the Coliseums of the modern age.

It must be borne in mind that gladiators were slaves, and that to call a man a gladiator in ancient Rome was the equivalent of calling him a gaol-bird and a black-guard at once. Victorian novelists may have done their best to throw an aura of heroism over the gladiatorial schools, but in reality they were a degradation, not a calling. The gladiator might be a criminal sentenced to death in the arena or a German prisoner-of-war, glad of the chance to fight for his life until he had scraped together perhaps enough to buy his freedom, in preference to a life of menial misery in the slave establishment of some big farm. Gladiators were organized in small barracks, where they were knocked into shape for the arena and generally subjected to a stern and harsh discipline under the *lanista* or manager, who was not infrequently their owner. The *lanista* hired them out and paired them off, as occasion arose. When a big show was impending the agents of the magistrate who was giving or organizing it would go round to visit the leading *lanistae*, and a programme would be drawn up. Such programmes were often posted up in advance in public places, and specimens of them, painted up on house-walls, can still be seen in Pompeii.

In the arena gladiators commonly fought in pairs. It was a bitter and brutal life. They might have to fight against a picked swordsman of unknown quantity from another school, and it might be to the death, or against a comrade of the same school and perhaps kill him or be killed by him. Contests followed set types. A good swordsman would most commonly be made into a " Samnite " with a fighting equipment consisting of a visored and crested helmet, a large oblong shield of the legionary pattern, a metal-studded leather guard on his sword-arm and a metal greave on the left leg (which would be more exposed to attack than the other), and the short, stabbing sword.   Another type of swordsman was the *murmillo*, so called from the crest fashioned in the shape of a fish which he wore on his helmet.   The " Thracian " was armed with a small shield (usually round) and a curved sword.   A man of a nimble, athletic type, fast on his legs, would be made into a " net-man " (*retiarius*).   His main armament was a net with which his aim was to entangle his opponent and pull him down.   He had no protective armour beyond leg-thongs, an arm-guard and perhaps a neck-guard of leather, and no other weapon beyond a trident and a small dagger tucked into his waist-band.   The trident was a three-pronged spear-fork given him more for ornament than for use; the trident was an ancient fishing-spear, the regular attribute of the sea-gods Poseidon and Neptune, and with the net would make the *retiarius* look like a fantastic fisherman.   The *retiarius* fought against a swordsman (in this contest called the " pursuer," *secutor*, for the main part of the net-man's tactics was to tire his opponent out by running away from him) armed much in the Samnite way described above.   At first sight it would appear that the odds were heavily in favour of the *secutor*, but in practice this proved untrue.   The net-man, with his finely-meshed net which he could with one movement cast and gather back into a ball, was a sinister and dreaded adversary.

These and other types drawn from different national-ities and styles of fighting (Gauls, Africans, Germans) were matched against each other in varied pairs.   Con-tests between armed horsemen and charioteers were also staged, and sometimes mimic battles between bands of armed men.   Often fights with wooden or blunt weapons were put on to begin the programme before the serious business began.

Bloodshed and killings were the order of the day; often, as Seneca says, it was sheer murder. But lives were frequently spared. If a gladiator went down or was seriously wounded he raised a finger of his left hand to entreat the president of the games and the crowd for mercy. If he had fought bravely spectators would wave handkerchiefs and napkins to obtain reprieve; if they were dissatisfied with his performance they gestured with down-turned thumbs for him to be despatched by his opponent. The dead were dragged off by attendants, and the next item on the programme would come on.

Gladiatorial shows of an exceptional kind were the sham naval battles (*naumachiae*) staged on lakes. Caesar gave one in 46 B.C. in a huge artificial basin in the Campus Martius, in which two fleets took part, each manned by 3,000 captives and convicts. In 2 B.C. Augustus staged a gladiatorial " Salamis " with " Persians " fighting against " Athenians." There were similar shows in the reigns of Claudius, Titus and Domitian, that in the reign of Claudius being conspicuous for the fact that the crews were on this occasion not required to fight to the death.

Though enthusiastically applauded and indeed demanded by the populace, such entertainments were not to the taste of all Romans. Tacitus condemns Tiberius's son Drusus for his addiction to gladiatorial games, and the following passage of Seneca is eloquent on the demoralizing effect they inevitably had.

" There is nothing so detrimental to character as to attend a public entertainment. For there under the guise of pleasure vice the more easily creeps in. You wonder no doubt what I mean. I mean that I come back the greedier, the more grasping, the more wanton, worse still, the more cruel and inhuman because I have mixed with my fellow-men. I happened to look in at a midday show, expecting to find some sport and fun, a little relaxation from the sight of human blood. It was just the reverse. In the old days they showed mercy. Now they cut out such trifling and get down to manslaughter pure and simple. The combatants have no armour; their whole body is exposed for the stroke, and they never thrust in vain. The mob prefers it to regular duels and picked matches. Why not? There is no helmet or shield to keep off the blade. What is the use of armour? What is the use of skill? Such things serve only to delay the stroke of death. In the morning men are thrown to lions and bears; in the afternoon they are at the mercy of the spectators. The mob clamours for the slayers to be slain in turn; the victor is merely marked down to provide another death. For the contestant death is the only release; fire and the sword is the order of the day."

THE THEATRE

Plays were given at Rome at each of the four great festivals, as well as on the occasion of triumphs and funeral celebrations and on other public holidays. By the beginning of the second century B.C., we are told, no fewer than forty-eight days in the year were available for official scenic productions. Before theatres were built expressly for the purpose, plays were performed in the circus or on temporary stages in front of extemporized wooden seating at the foot of the Palatine or one of the other hills. Rome's first theatre, built of stone and marble, was given by Pompey in 55 B.C. and was restored by Augustus. It was situated at the southern end of the Campus Martius and held some 10,000 spectators. The year 13 B.C. saw the dedication of two other theatres, that of Balbus, slightly smaller than Pompey's, and the noble structure, which is still one of the most impressive sights of Rome, called the theatre of Marcellus in honour of Augustus's nephew who died in 23 B.C. Both these were situated farther to the south, near the river.

Plays were given in the main by the State, the aediles contracting for the purpose with proprietors of stage companies, and had officially begun in 240 B.C., when the conclusion of the First Punic War was celebrated by a tragedy and a comedy adapted from the Greek by Livius Andronicus, a Greek who had come to Rome as a prisoner in the course of the war against Tarentum. The historian Livy traces the origins of Roman drama to a much earlier date, to the year 364 B.C., when he says actors were introduced from Etruria. These actors apparently did little but gesticulate gracefully to the accompaniment of strains from the flute, and performed a sort of rudimentary dumb-show or pantomimic dance. With this the youth of Rome combined verbal badinage in the style of the old Fescennine verses, a sort of ribald doggerel backchat originating in country festivals. The result was a dramatic medley with dialogue but without a plot. Plays with plots were Greek, and such were the plays introduced to Rome by Livius Andronicus— adaptations of Greek tragedies and comedies of mature and complex form. For the bulk of the populace, however, this Greek drama was too highbrow. It was left to the professionals, and the young men kept up the native tradition of ribald dialogue without plot. Their performances, which gradually improved in literary finish, came to be used, like the French harlequinade, as short tail-pieces at productions of the more formal play and were called *exodia*. Much of their inspiration was drawn from another form of native drama found in Campania called the Atellane play, a sketch-comedy of stock types reminiscent of our Punch and Judy. Its types were Pappus the old dotard, Bucco the blabbing dunce, Maccus the glutton and braggart, Dossenus the sly wiseacre hunchback and various bogies and monsters with hideous masks, calculated to make the village infant shrink in terror to his mother's bosom, says Juvenal. Even when Naevius had founded a Roman tragedy and Plautus and Terence had raised comedy to brilliant heights, *exodia* on the native pattern were still produced and retained their popularity well into the imperial age.

Similar to the *exodia* were the performances called Mimes, realistic short sketches of low life in vulgar vein, not unlike the sketches which find a regular place today in music-hall variety programmes; but these enjoyed the advantage of not using masks. The Mimes derived entirely from Greek sources in South Italy, but achieved great vogue in Rome and like the *exodia* enjoyed an extensive revival in the last century B.C., when a new interest in Italian, as opposed to strictly Roman, products set in after the Social War. Such performances were not officially encouraged, and there is a story that Julius Caesar condemned a knight, one Decimus Laberius, to appear in one of his own low productions, and so to lose his knightly rank, as a punishment for authorship so degrading.

Such dramatic forms were the side-lines of Roman

drama and can hardly be compared with the main body; but their persistent popularity points to the fact that the formal drama never effectively rooted itself in Rome. The reason is not far to seek. The formal drama was not a natural growth but imposed from without on Greek models, and public taste never rose to it. During the third and second centuries B.C., a great body of Roman tragedies, historical plays and comedies was produced, but it is significant that with the exception of six plays of Terence and twenty-one plays of Plautus, all comedies, only fragments have survived. Both Plautus and Terence based their plays on Greek plays, adapting plots and dialogue without scruple. Plautus's comedies are vigorously-written comedies of manners with a good admixture of slapstick and a rough vein of humour more to the taste of the Roman public than the more elegant and more subtle compositions of Terence written under the patronage of a Hellenizing circle and appealing to a more sophisticated audience. A very rough modern equivalent of the plays of these two dramatists would be the Aldwych farces of Ben Travers and Ralph Lynn written in the style of Restoration comedy. The love of a young man of good family for a courtesan, who may be a gentle-born lady after all, his difficulties with a tyrannical father, the tricks of an artful slave who solves the problem—such were the typical contents of these comedies. Their characters included the miser, the stingy usurer, the cringing parasite, the braggart soldier, the nice girl and the hussy. Here are the titles of some of Plautus's plays: *The Ghost, The Pot of Gold, The Threepenny Piece, The Boasting Warrior, The Prisoners.* His play *The Menaechmus Brothers* served as a basis for Shakespeare's *Comedy of Errors*, much of which will give an idea of the typical Plautine plot. Terence uses much the same characters in subtler, more cultured textures. His *Woman of Andros* is a story which Thornton Wilder has converted into a modern novel. Under the Empire drama continued to be written by literary aspirants, but tragedy tended to be recited before private audiences, and public performances became increasingly revivals of old masterpieces. Tragedy was gradually superseded by pantomimes, more elaborate and reputable than the low-class mime of which we have spoken. These, which exploited all the arts of music, décor and dancing, had themes frequently taken from romantic mythology more or less serious in vein (sometimes scenes from well-known tragedies were adapted for the purpose) and were in some respects comparable with the modern romantic musical comedy and certain types of revue.

The dress of the actors varied with the type of performance. Tragedy took over Greek costume, the tragic robe with long sleeves, the high-soled buskin and by about 100 B.C. the mask. The Roman national and historical drama, the *fabulae togatae* and *praetextae*, naturally took the Roman tunic and toga. Instead of the high buskin comedy had its characteristic footwear the *soccus* or low slipper (hence Milton's reference to "Jonson's learned Sock"). As in Greek comedy, dress was many-coloured—purples, yellows and reds. Before about 100 B.C., when masks came into regular use, set-type wigs were used: the young man had a black wig, the old men white, slaves invariably red (a colour still favoured by modern comedians). Mime, essentially the most realistic dramatic type and played without masks, was played in the dress of real life.

Actors were in early times despised in Rome, were classed with gladiators, and could not possess citizen status; but during the last century B.C. the ban came to be lifted and distinguished actors achieved social recognition. Such was the celebrated comic actor Roscius, who was a friend of Cicero and became proverbial for his art. Women might act in mime (Antony's mistress Cytheris was a well-known actress), but on the legitimate stage, as in Shakespeare's theatre, female parts were taken by men and boys until late in the imperial age. The general apparatus of the Greek theatre was used, often vulgarized, as were other borrowings from Greece. The production of a Greek masterpiece might at times serve little purpose but as a vehicle for the display of booty from some great general's triumph. The 600 mules dragged into the performance of a *Clytemnestra* or the 3,000 mixing-bowls displayed in *The Trojan Horse*, ridiculed by Cicero, were but modest extravagances compared with others.

It is the purely secular pomp of the State dramatic performances at Rome, as contrasted with the religious sincerity and artistic depth of the Athenian, which betrays the superficiality of Roman drama. Pompey's theatre was a tribute to his sense of importance and a vehicle for personal display. Social distinctions were rigidly observed. The level space of the *orchestra* was reserved for senators, the first fourteen rows of the auditorium proper for knights, the commons sat above; boxes over the entrances on both sides were reserved for the presiding magistrate, the Imperial House and the Vestal Virgins. Lavish incidentals were used to pander to the crowd; we hear of sprinklings of perfume and of awnings spangled with stars to represent the sky.

ATHLETICS

For athletics as we know them, contests in running, wrestling, boxing and the like, the Roman had little use. They were Greek and were for the most part despised as the entertainment of a dilettante race, and, no doubt, the average Roman felt them poor sport after the strong meat of his own chariot-races and gladiatorial games. The Emperor Nero owed his fall in some measure to the unpopularity which he incurred by his personal attempts to establish Greek athletic and artistic competitions in Rome. So long as the contests were enacted by Greek athletes imported for the purpose they were tolerated as an interesting and occasional novelty; the first recorded occasion of such an exhibition was in 186 B.C., and similar exhibitions were staged by Sulla, Pompey and Caesar, and Augustus went so far as to establish at Nicopolis on the Epirote coast near the site of his victory at Actium a series of athletic and musical contests on the lines of the Olympian Games. Athletic games appear in the reigns of Gaius and Claudius without attracting undue notice. It was when Nero, notorious for his personal dilettantism in various forms of Greek artistic and athletic activity, sought to establish a cult of Greek athletics among the young men of Rome and himself appeared as performer in public that revulsion set in. Juvenal and other writers of the time are contemptuous and sarcastic, and to the end of the Empire Roman opinion persisted in the view that to take part in public competition in athletics was a degrading activity and best left to foreigners.

The cult of Exercise never in Rome reached the importance it has today. If a man wanted to keep fit he went regularly to the baths; there he could play ball and run, if he wished, in a quite informal way; if he were particularly hearty he could run and do exercises in the Campus Martius and swim in the fast-running Tiber.

THE BATHS

The baths to a Roman meant far more than the term itself might imply. It meant bathing, exercise and, above all, company. The baths were the place where one met people, where one spent a whole morning or a whole afternoon. The baths were the club-house of the ancient world. The most prominent baths were of amazing size and elaboration, as anyone who has walked through the gigantic ruins of Caracalla's Baths at Rome will know. And there were baths all over the Roman world from the Tyne (where the neatly-alcoved changing room can still be seen at Chesters) to the Saharan Desert; in Rome itself there were hundreds.

The first function of a Roman bath was to provide what we know as a Turkish bath with varying degrees of heat. In early baths heating was by means of charcoal braziers, and baths of this type were available for public use from the end of the third century B.C. Soon after the beginning of the first century B.C. a new process, the hypocaust, was introduced, by which hot air was circulated under the floor of a room and up the walls through flue tiles. To effect this, the floor of the room was supported on rows of short pillars round which the hot air was forced from an adjoining furnace (see page 92). By this device the temperature in the tepid room and in the hot room could be regulated, and from these the bather would pass to the cold plunge. But

varying degrees and sequences were possible in elabor-
ately-arranged baths.   Rooms for dressing and un-
dressing, for massage and anointing, for games and
exercise, for wine-drinking and refreshments, even halls
for meetings and lectures and libraries, would have
their place.

Small bath-establishments were run by private proprietors and managers who might rent them for a period
as a speculative concern ; large baths were run by the
State. Admission fees were small, and there were
exclusive establishments to cater for class and sex distinctions.   Some baths had duplicate provision for men
and women; some kept special times for women; but
mixed bathing seems to have been prevalent, though
officially discouraged, as Martial inveighs against women
who bathe in inadequate costumes.

The philosopher Seneca once had lodgings over some
baths and has left in one of his letters a vivid account of
the various noises that beset his ears from below:

> ". . . the hearties swinging weights and grunting
> and blowing . . . somebody being rubbed down, the
> smack of hands on flesh . . . the chant of the scorers
> at the ball-game . . . the uproar when a thief is
> caught in the act . . . the man who likes the sound of
> his own voice in the bath . . . the fellows who dive
> in and hit the water with a resounding splash . . .
> the cries of the cake-seller, the sausage-man and the
> pastry-man, all hawking their wares in their own
> peculiar notes . . ."

And in more serious vein (the noises, he says, he can get
used to) he deplores the growing standards of luxury,
contrasting the simple baths of earlier times with the
elaborate structures of his own day.

PLATE XXI.—A ROMAN PROVINCIAL CITY.
Paved road leading to the Arch of Trajan, Timgad.

PLATE XXII.—HADRIAN'S WALL, IN ROMAN BRITAIN.

View near Housesteads. The wall, originally 18–20 feet high, runs 73 miles from the Tyne to the Solway.

" Today a man thinks himself poor and unclean unless the walls gleam with large and costly mirrors, unless Numidian inlay sets off Alexandrian marble, unless their surrounds are faced all round with intricate patterns with all the colour range of paintings, unless the ceiling-domes are a mass of glass, unless our swimming-pools are lined with Thasian marble (once a rare sight in any temple), unless the water is poured in through silver valves . . . So we progress; establishments which once drew admiring crowds are classed as antiques, once luxury has elaborated some new device, to her own defeat."

CHAPTER IX

SCIENCE AND KNOWLEDGE

" . . . *Excudent alii spirantia mollius aera*
(credo equidem) et vivos ducent de marmore vultus;
orabunt causas melius, caelique meatus
describent radio et surgentia sidera dicent :
tu regere imperio populos, Romane, memento
(hae tibi erunt artes), pacisque imponere morem,
parcere subiectis et debellare superbos. . . ."—VIRGIL.

" Others, I deem, shall work the breathing bronze to softer forms; others shall from marble draw faces to the very life; shall plead their causes with readier tongue; shall trace with the rod of wisdom the courses of the heaven and tell the risings of the stars; the Roman's heed shall be to guide the nations under his dominion, to set on the world the habit of peace, to spare the humbled and war down the proud."

SO sings the Roman laureate of the Augustan age, a trifle wistfully perhaps, for he was a man of high culture who had been trained in schools inspired by Hellenic ideals. But he saw that his countrymen had the merits of their defects; if they were not born artists or thinkers, they were born to rule and so provide the broader aspects of a world peace. ·The truth is that the Romans were never more than amateurs in science. Any credit which they deserve in the history of science attaches to their work as preservers not as originators. It requires a fine mind to know a good thing in the world of the spirit when it sees it, and though Rome adopted and handed down to history much of the Greek achievement in science, there was much which slipped and was lost betwixt cup and lip. *Nostri omnium utilitatium et virtutum rapacissimi* (" we are gluttons for the useful

and the good ") wrote the learned Pliny; but the order
of the words is revealing. Utility came first, and that is
not the spirit which will safeguard the life of science.
A modern writer writes severely: " The Romans were
not apt scholars. To their failure it is largely due that
it was only in the seventeenth century that western
European towns attained the degree of scientific culture
that had been achieved in Alexandria two thousand
years before."

The bulk of this chapter, then, must inevitably consist
in an epitome of the Greek scientific achievement as it
existed in the world taken over by Rome. Yet no
account of the Roman world can be complete without
such an epitome. For the Roman who had an interest
in such things there was a rich and solid body of knowledge awaiting him, and if Rome could not boast a
Euclid, an Archimedes or a Hero, she had her encyclo-
paedists and her learned amateurs, a Varro and an
elder Pliny.

What science could the world of his times offer to the
intelligent Roman of the first century A.D. ? Based on
modern standards a summary answer to this question
might run as follows:

Mathematics, viz. arithmetic, geometry and solid
geometry, conic sections and a little trigonometry:
excellent.
Physics: vague and rather backward, but with some
promising general ideas.
Chemistry: virtually non-existent.
Astronomy: on good mathematical foundations;
bright and promising, though still has far to go.
Geography: satisfactory; interesting and on the right
lines.
Medicine: very creditable and full of promise.

Botany and zoology: sound and well-developed.
Applied mathematics: a very fair grasp of essentials
in a limited field.

Mathematics is the oldest of the exact sciences. Arts
(such as astrology) based on some sort of mathematical
calculation are found in various civilizations of the
ancient world, among the Chinese, the Egyptians and
the Chaldeans, for example; but the Greeks may claim
the credit of putting such studies on a basis of strict
reason. It was in virtue of such an attitude that some
of the best minds of Greece, above all Plato, found in
mathematics the best of all educational subjects, because
its pursuit is at root purely intellectual, not dependent
on actual happenings, like the physical sciences, or on
particular words or writings, like the study of literature.
It is pure speculation, pure inquiry, complete in itself,
owning no allegiance to the outside world. That is
why it got its name. *Mathema* in Greek means " learning," and *mathematics* is learning par excellence.

Geometry is the form in which this pure mathematic
first appeared. This is easily understandable, for in
geometry we can see how the ideas of form and relation
are abstracted from the everyday world: the idea of a
right-angle is easily suggested by the simple process of
setting a stick in the ground in the way most likely to
make it stay stable, the idea of a triangle by the shadow
which it will cast in sunlight; and the art of building is
not likely to progress far until builders had succeeded in
grasping such ideas—the abstract idea of a right-angle
as something distinct from this particular fortuitous
right-angle, say, between doorpost and lintel. Pyramids
and temple pediments cannot be constructed before the
idea of the isosceles triangle has been conceived.

The term *geometry* means in the Greek the measurement of the earth, and we are given a good idea why it was so called by certain stories which are told about Thales, who lived in a Greek city in Asia Minor about 600 B.C., and was the first thinker who made geometry a scientific study. He was said to have taught the Egyptians how they could measure the height of their pyramids by calculations based on the measurements of their shadows, and further to have devised a system for measuring the distance of ships at sea. Yet this was still far from the thing we call geometry. Thales's results almost entirely consisted of isolated geometrical propositions whose proofs were merely deductive. A great advance was made some seventy years later by Pythagoras who lived in the South of Italy, the attachment of whose name to the forty-seventh theorem of the first book of Euclid has secured him a sure immortality. He was primarily a moralist and a philosopher and used mathematics merely as a background for his philosophic teaching, but he took geometry a step forward by relating it to the study of abstract number (or Arithmetic, which in Greek means the science of counting). For him geometry and arithmetic were inseparable, and for the rest of its history among the Greeks arithmetic was absorbed in geometry. Pythagoras's arithmetic, so far as it went, was concerned with the properties of number, integers (for fractions never concerned him) rather than with methods of calculation. He was much excited, for example, by the property of the number ten that it is the sum of 1 and 2 and 3 and 4; and the symbolic ten in the form of a triangle with its apex 1 and its base 4 integers was adopted by his school as a badge. Similarly he would call 9 a square number and 12 an oblong. But his most significant discovery is implied in the theorem called after him: that in a right-angled triangle the square on the hypotenuse (ἡ ὑποτείνουσα γραμμή, " the subtended line ") is equal to the sum of the squares on the other two sides. He further saw that in the isosceles right-angled triangle the relation of the hypotenuse to the other sides cannot be expressed in a simple numerical ratio. This incommensurability of the side of the square with the diagonal is a fact of vital importance in the development of mathematics, because in such a case there is no longer the alternative between expressing this relation concretely and leaving it as a conception; such a relation must remain an abstract: we call it a " surd."

After this beginning the study of geometry was extended both by the followers of Pythagoras and elsewhere in Greece, until, with the introduction of the ideas of planes and curves, the theory of the circle and solid geometry were worked out and the legitimate methods of geometrical proof were recognized. The great philosopher Plato (who flourished about the middle of the fourth century B.C. at Athens, where he founded his famous school the Academy) was also a great mathematician. Like Pythagoras he used mathematics as a sort of mystic background for his teaching, so much so that his pupil Aristotle (who was a biologist, not a mathematician) could complain that in his day mathematics had superseded philosophy. In Plato himself (who, inspired by his master Socrates, laid the foundations of modern Western philosophy) we find the explicit recognition that the spatial character of geometry is strictly irrelevant. He insists on the difference between geometrical and arithmetical proof, and a contemporary of his has left us a very interesting fragment in which he says, " I think that in respect of wisdom Arithmetic surpasses all the other arts and especially Geometry, since it treats the objects which it wants to study in a far clearer way." [1]

But it was in the third century B.C. that Greek mathematics reached its zenith. The new university of Alexandria founded at the end of the fourth century was largely responsible for this advance, and with its schools are associated the three great names of Euclid, Apollonius and Archimedes. It was Euclid who set out in a clear logical method the chief theorems of plane and solid geometry and in fact formulated the body of elementary geometry on which mathematical teaching in schools depends to this day. Text-books as familiar as those of Hall and Knight and Durell are little more than annotated editions of Euclid. Apollonius of Perga expounded conic sections, and in modern times, to mention but two names, Kepler and Isaac Barrow owed a great debt to him. Kepler was able to develop his contributions to astronomy only because of the spade-work done by Apollonius. Isaac Barrow was the Cambridge scholar who, significantly enough, was Professor of Greek and exchanged his Chair for that of Mathematics as soon as that post was instituted; and it was he who taught Newton. Archimedes stands out as the greatest genius of them all. We know him chiefly, no doubt, from the principle of Archimedes in hydrostatics and from the Eureka story. There are several similar stories of his mechanical inventiveness, how, for instance, he contrived by the use of giant mirrors to burn the sails of the Roman ships besieging Syracuse in his time and made

[1] Quoted by Burnet, *Greek Philosophy from Thales to Plato*, p. 323.

new and mighty engines of defence which kept the Romans at bay. He may be said to have founded the sciences of statics and hydrostatics; but he also made some vital contributions to the theory of pure mathematics, particularly in connection with the circle, spirals and the surfaces and volumes of figures.

Greek mathematics continued to flourish under the Roman Empire and it was in this age that two new branches of the subject were originated. It is usual to ascribe the invention of Algebra to the Arabs; it is true that the decimal system which they developed and the all-important zero point are now integral to this science, but the science in its essentials had been virtually established by the Greek Diophantus in an elaborate treatise produced in the middle of the third century A.D. Similarly in the work of the astronomers Hipparchus, Menelaus and of the geographer-astronomer Ptolemy, stretching from the second century B.C. to the second century A.D., we find the rudiments of trigonometry.

On the side of physics the achievement of ancient science is by no means so considerable. Physicists there had been since the first stirrings of philosophical curiosity in Ionia; but with certain exceptions Greek physics, as seen by modern eyes, suffered from the fatal circumstance that it was not distinguished from philosophy at large. In such an inquiry specialization must come before depth is achieved. The first physicists were clever and ingenious men, but they were obsessed with the object of *explaining* the world. For physics to be possible they had first to *describe* it. The ultimate physical constituent of the world, said Thales, is water. No, said Anaximenes, it is air. No, said Heraclitus, it is fire. It is all three, said Empedocles, and added a

fourth, " earth." He also maintained the theory that
" Love " and " Strife " (i.e. the principles of Attraction
and Reaction) were the elemental forces of the Universe.
All these theories were bright ideas, each capable of
ingenious defence, and each has its place in a thorough-
going physic, but as thus simply enunciated they remained for the most part clever guesses, not substantial
enough to satisfy a thorough mind. To achieve more
satisfying results two ways were open. One could either
dismiss such half-scientific explanations of the world as
alien to logic and pursue in their place a purely spiritual
theory of the universe; or one could descend from the
philosopher's chair and apply oneself to a sober scrutiny
of the things one wanted to explain. Plato chose the
former course; Aristotle chose the latter. Aristotle it was
who founded the precise activity which we know as
science and gave the world the laboratory and the bench;
though he was himself primarily a biologist he distinguished the field of physics from that of the other sciences.
In a masterly fashion he showed what his predecessors
had been trying to do in the world of science by his
analysis of the four types of causation. They all have
their place: the water, air, fire, earth of the Ionians as
material causes; the Love and Strife of Empedocles as
efficient causes; the number-relations of the Pythagoreans
emphasized the mathematical structure of matter; the
Platonic insistence that any true science must show that
the universe is ordered by an underlying, all-inclusive
purpose points to the importance of the *final* (to use the
Aristotelian term, the teleological) cause.

One memorable physical theory with which the educated Roman would be familiar from the lines of
Lucretius is the atomic theory, first formulated by the

Greeks Leucippus and Democritus five centuries before Christ. According to this theory matter consists of minute particles, infinite in number, conjoined in various and ever-changing combinations, existing in the void. Their collisions and changes produce the changes of our physical world. This theory, with its startling repercussions on the realm of ethics and religion (for what place is there for Providence and Free Will in a universe subject to so mechanical a law?), has lived into our present day and beneath all the refinements of modern research can still be recognized in its essentials.

It is commonly maintained that Greek science was one-sided in that it was deductive and did not proceed by experiment. When we make allowances for handicaps in the absence of flexible notations and material equipment, there is little to be said for such a judgement. It may be true of the earliest pioneers of science, but it is not true of the great names. We have only to think of the clinical methods of the school of Hippocrates, of the patient methods of Aristotle in his zoology, of the brilliant water-clock experiment by which Empedocles proved that air and empty space are different things, of the science of hydrostatics founded on experiment by Archimedes.

Of chemistry there is little to be said. It had hardly yet been born, but its development had been foreshadowed as far back as the fifth century B.C. when Anaxagoras, the friend of Pericles, asked how it was that the food which a man ate was converted into flesh and blood, bone and sinew, skin and hair and went on to ask, still more pregnantly, how it was possible unless bread itself somehow contained the elements of flesh and blood and the bodily components. No doubt the manufacturing processes, such as existed in such countries as Egypt, dyeing, tanning, glass-making, would stimulate some application to the minor practical problems of chemistry involved; but the Roman Empire could show no general awareness of the subject.

Botany and zoology had had their learned Greek specialists, and, even beside modern achievements, the ancient knowledge and accuracy is impressive. In this sphere, as we can see from the elder Pliny's work, there were Romans who took a keen amateur interest, as was natural when large country estates were so prized; but there were no Roman scientists.

Of all the " liberal " sciences, that which touched the Roman most nearly was astronomy. His term for it was *astrologia*, which implies that he made little or no distinction between astronomy and its mystical applications to the destinies of men. Further to commend it, there was the undeniable fact that accurate calendar-making, an important matter for the statesman, depended on a true interpretation of astronomical phenomena. But here again it was the practical applications, not the theory, which interested the Roman. For the individual student who might be interested in theory Greek science had various alternatives to offer. He might follow the system of Eudoxus, who held that the heavenly bodies revolve round the earth in various concentric spheres (a theory from which the charming fantasy of the music of the spheres takes its origin); or that of Heraclides, who held that the sun and the planets revolve round the earth, with the exception of Venus and Mercury which revolve round the sun, and that the earth rotates on its own axis; or he might prefer the teachings of those who held that all five planets revolve round the sun; or he might master the elaborate theory of epicycles by which the great astronomer Hipparchus explained the variations in the planetary orbits; and lastly he could believe, as we do, that the earth and the planets revolve round the sun. For, though it found little favour with the experts of the ancient world, such a theory had been propounded as long before as the middle of the third century B.C. by Aristarchus of Samos. Substantially right, Aristarchus's theory as stated by him lacked the refinements and precision required to explain the planetary phenomena and needed the genius of a Copernicus to elaborate it before it reached a fully acceptable form.

A passage from the elder Pliny's *Natural History* (here quoted in Philemon Holland's inimitable translation) will serve to illustrate the sort of interest which an intelligent Roman gentleman of the early imperial age might take in the cosmology of the day:

" The first and principal thing that offers itself to be considered is the figure of the Earth, in which by a general consent we all agree. For we speak of the round ball of the earth and confess that it is a globe enclosed within two poles. Yet the form is not of a perfect and absolute roundel, considering such a great height of hills and such plains of downs. But if the compass were taken by lines, the ends of those lines would meet exactly in circuit and prove the figure of a just circle. The heaven bends and inclines toward the centre, but the earth goes from the centre, while the world with continual volubility and turning about drives the huge and excessive globe into the form of a round ball.

" There is much ado and great debate between learned men and contrariwise between those of the lewd and ignorant multitude, for they hold that men are spread over all parts of the earth and stand one against another, foot to foot, so that the Zenith or point of the Heavens is even and alike unto all; in whatever part they are they tread after the same manner on the middle of the earth.   But the common sort ask the question, How it happens that the people just opposite against us do not fall off into Heaven ? As if there were not a question also ready whether those on the opposite side should marvel why we fall not down.   Now there is a reason, carrying a probability even to the multitude, that on an uneven and unequal globe of the Earth, with many ascents and degrees (as if the figure resembled a Pineapple) it may be well enough inhabited all over in every place. But what good does all this do, when another wonder as great as it arises, namely, that the globe itself hangs and yet does not fall together with us ?   As if the power of that Spirit especially which is enclosed in the World were doubted: or that anything could fall, especially when Nature is repugnant thereto and affords no place whither to fall."

Such, no doubt, was the conversation which might have been heard at the dinner-tables of Pliny and his friends. The time was not yet ripe when the fall of the apple should move Newton to formulate the astonishingly simple theory which today we take for granted; but we can see that in the ancient world the interests of men were marshalled and their feet well set on the paths of speculative inquiry.

From cosmology to geography is no long cry, and geography, with its obvious practical side, was another subject likely to appeal to the Roman.   How far the bounds of the known world extended for the Roman of the Augustan age will be clear from the sketch of the Roman world given in the next chapter.   Latterly, the course of conquest had been opening up the edges of unknown lands: Julius Caesar pushing north through Gaul and over the Ocean to the unkempt island of Britain, and Pompey in the course of his Eastern campaigns opening up Armenia to the Caucasus, kept alive the general interest in exploration. The reign of Augustus saw much of hitherto unknown Switzerland opened up and most of the country between North Italy and the Middle and Upper Danube, in the work of consolidating the Northern frontier. In the reign of Augustus, too, Cornelius Balbus reached Fezzan and there were several attempts to penetrate to the sources of that great and mysterious river, the Nile. Soon Drusus in his attempts to solve the problem of the Northern frontier was to push into Germany to the Elbe and Denmark, and, in the reign of Claudius, Suetonius Paulinus in the work of pacifying the annexed Mauretania penetrated beyond the Atlas Mountains.

In its beginning Greek geography had been, as Roman geography always was, purely empirical. The Greeks had always been voyagers. Their homelands were hard, and a living from the produce of earth was not easily come by; on the other hand the sea was inviting. Creeping into the much-indented coast-line, the sea was friendly and offered fish in plenty. There were plenty of harbours, calm weather that could be relied on in the summer months from April to October; there were the encouraging Etesian winds and there were few dangerous currents and no tides; and there was plenty of timber for the building of boats. Land-scarcity and political unrest in the cities gave a continual impetus to colonization from the earliest times. Added to these influences were the factors of commercial gain, for which the

Greek (as the Roman was never tired of remarking) had a ready eye, and of an innate and inexhaustible curiosity. In such a milieu geographical advance was inevitable. Yet looking back we must remember the obstacles which impeded the progress of geographical science. Ships were small and slightly-rigged and sail-manipulation in its crude infancy; there were no compasses; there were no means of storing food and water for long voyages; and no means of accurate mensuration. In spite of these handicaps exploration went steadily on, till it received a tremendous impetus in the great expedition of Alexander in the East. Not the least significant phase of this expedition was the employment of *bematistai* ("steppers" or, as we should say, "surveyors") whose office it was to calculate distances by standard paces. With the founding of Alexandria geography developed new scientific foundations. Mathematicians strove with the accurate formulation of longitudes and latitudes and to bring into line with them the knowledge gained from the reports of sea-captains and travellers' tales.

The fifth-century philosopher Parmenides had conceived of the earth as divided into frigid, temperate and torrid girdles or zones, and a crude idea of a meridian can be seen in Herodotus's history, when in connecting the mouths of the Danube and the Nile he draws a straight line between them which passes through Sinope and Cilicia Tracheia. Aristotle, who is the father of scientific geography as of so many sciences, defined Parmenides's ideas more accurately and formulated the extent of the temperate zone between the torrid and the arctic circle much on the lines of modern geography. Shortly after this time Pytheas of Marseilles undertook a famous voyage in the northern seas and in the course of his observations produced data from which a number of parallels of latitude were successfully established. That was soon after Alexander's campaigns had opened up the East. Within a few years Dicaearchus had constructed a map containing a median of latitude running from the Straits of Gibraltar in the West to the Hindu Kush in the East. In the second half of the next century Eratosthenes constructed a geographical system in which physical and mathematical geography and topographical knowledge were combined to a single end. When we have made allowance for his errors and ignorance (he thought that the Caspian joined up with the Northern Ocean and had no conception of the southward extension of Africa and of India), the resultant map of the central land-mass is a striking achievement. The further researches of Hipparchus (whose work in astronomy we have already mentioned) carried the great work of Eratosthenes to a further degree of accuracy in the mapping of Europe.

Coming to Roman times we find Polybius, the historian of the Punic Wars, devoting a book of his work to geography as an influence on history. The enlightened way in which he introduces geographical factors as essential to the true understanding of history marks a new advance in the human application of the subject, and when the Stoic teacher and traveller Posidonius in the course of his encyclopaedic learning turned mathematical calculation to the service of descriptive geography he found a ready public in the intelligentsia of Rome.

There were no great Roman geographers. Cicero, who when he was not being the Roman Demosthenes liked to think of himself alternately as the Roman

PLATE XXIII.—A ROMAN FORT IN BRITAIN.

Hardknot Castle, a commanding site in Cumberland: an imaginary reconstruction. Below the fort is the bath-house; to the right is the parade ground.

PLATE XXIV.—ROMAN LETTERING.

An inscription, very finely cut (the letters are eight inches high), from Uroconium (Wroxeter), a Roman city near Shrewsbury. The full text runs IMP(ERATORI) CAES(ARI) DIVI TRAIANI PARTHICI FIL(IO) DIVI NERVAE NEPOTI TRAIANO HADRIANO AUG(USTO) PONTIFICI MAXIMO TRIB(UNICIAE) POT(ESTATI) XIIII CO(N)S(ULI) III P(ATRIAE) CIVITAS CORNOVIORUM ("To the Emperor, Caesar, son of the deified Trajanus Parthicus, grandson of the deified Nerva, Trajanus Hadrianus Augustus, Pontifex Maximus, in the fourteenth year of his reign, thrice Consul, Father of his Country, the community of the Cornovii (erected this) ").

Aristotle and the Roman Plato, thought of writing a book on geography, but thought better of it when he saw the mathematics with which Greek geography was wrapped up. The first Roman work on geography, that of Pomponius Mela (who lived in the reign of Claudius), was merely a popular handbook, thin and of little merit. The elder Pliny a little later in the century included four books on geography in his *Natural History*, but they are no more than a dull and learned digest of names and travellers' stories and curiosities.

"Near those Scythians that live toward the Arctic pole, and not far from that climate which is under the rising of the North-East wind, about that famous cave or hole out of which that wind is said to issue (which place they call the cloister or key of the earth) dwell the Arimaspians who are known for having one eye only in the midst of their foreheads. They carry on a war about the gold mines with Griffins, a kind of wild beast that flies and fetches gold out of the veins of those mines. These savage beasts strive as eagerly to keep and hold the gold mines as the Arimaspians to get the gold away from them.

"Above them are other Scythians called Anthropophagi, in a country called Abarimon within a vale of Mount Imaus, savage and wild men, living and conversing usually among the brute beasts; they have their feet growing backward and turned behind the calves of their legs, although they run most swiftly. These men can live in no other climate than their own, which is the reason they cannot be brought to other kings that border upon them, nor could they be brought to Alexander the Great. . . ."

And so on. Pliny was an ardent and painstaking amateur of learning and, as the event proved, was to

13

give his life for his zest for knowledge (he was Prefect of the Roman fleet on the Misenum station at the time of the great eruption of Vesuvius and, sailing in in his anxiety to investigate this remarkable phenomenon, there met his death); but he was not a scientist. The historian Tacitus writing a biography of his father-in-law Agricola and wishing to explain the phenomenon of the Midnight Sun betrays a lack of geographical knowledge of which an intelligent Greek student might well have been ashamed. The work of Strabo, now the greatest work of ancient descriptive geography which we have, was scarcely known to the Roman world of his day (the age of Augustus). In comparison with this great work, the short treatise of Pomponius Mela, written in the reign of Claudius, the only extant Latin work written expressly on the subject, is dull and paltry. The *Germania* of Tacitus, written at a time when the work of the Flavian emperors in strengthening the connected Rhine-Danube frontier was directing attention to the tribes of the North, has little authoritativeness as a geographical work. It is the work of an amateur, in which the spirit of the scientific researcher is almost wholly absent.

Maps of a sort were not lacking; though the idea of a spherical earth was by the end of the first century B.C. generally accepted, plane maps of the known world seem to have been in common use. Such must have been the map which Agrippa caused to be set on a wall of the Porticus Vipsania and that which appeared engraved on a wall in the Forum of Vespasian some two centuries later. That small maps were a common article of private possession is suggested by the passage in Propertius in which a wife scans a map as she thinks of her soldier-husband away in the East. Many of the purposes for which we now use maps were for the Romans served by itineraries and diagrams in which lists of towns and distances were more important than geographical proportions. Such was in effect the famous Peutinger Table, a coloured diagrammatic map of the late Empire, giving towns, roads and distances, as seen in a mediaeval copy. Sometimes elaborate tables of distances were set up on milestones. The most famous example of this is the Golden Milestone of Augustus, which is mentioned in Chapter X. The fusion between mathematics and utility such as gave us Mercator's projection had yet to be made.

MEDICINE

The first doctor to come to Rome, according to Pliny the Elder, was one Agatharchus, who came from Greece in 219 B.C., and was set up by the State as a practitioner with every symbol of respect. " They say that he was a surgeon and for a time much appreciated, but that soon his rigorous use of knife and cautery earned the name of butcher and brought his art and all doctors into ill repute." This was seventy-two years after the cult of the Greek god of healing, Aesculapius, had been introduced to Rome and set up on the island in the Tiber; so that the Romans seem to have been prepared to take advantage of Greek discoveries in medicine from the time of their first continuing contacts with the Greek states of the south.

The doctors of Rome remained Greeks. Cato the die-hard might pour contempt on the tribe and their devices, might ironically suggest that they were the agents of a conspiracy to destroy all barbarians. All he could recommend as alternatives were the primitive combination of herbal lore and mumbo-jumbo which had survived from a timeless past.

But enlightenment prevailed, and the Greeks had come to stay. Julius Caesar held out Roman citizenship to the Greek physicians of Rome. Under the early Empire they were similarly encouraged. Greek doctors flourish and assume Roman names. Specialists spring up. Nursing-homes are established, not only those on large estates for the care of the slave-establishment, but small private homes run by doctors. Medical care in time ceases to be the monopoly of those rich enough to possess slave-doctors; towns throughout the Empire come to appoint municipal physicians, and the army medical service is steadily developed.

This is not the place to describe the development of the theory and practice of Greek medicine. Suffice it to say that it constituted one of the most conspicuous chapters of the Greek achievement. The father of the science was Hippocrates, who set it on a sound physical basis in the middle of the fifth century B.C., and founded a great school. Pre-eminently we owe to him the clinical method, the systematic recording of symptoms and patients' condition from day to day. His too was the famous oath administered to all the students who passed through the school whereby the young doctor swore to regard his calling as a sacred trust, never to use it for an unworthy end and never to betray a confidence which he might have received in pursuit of his calling. Thus among a race never conspicuous for good faith the profession of medicine was set on a high level of morality from the first. It is surprising and impressive that the familiar question, " Should a doctor tell ? " should have been first asked and answered in the negative by a Greek. Knowledge of anatomy and physiology grew steadily under state patronage in Hellenistic times. Looking today at an array of ancient medical instruments in a museum, we are amazed to find the lancets and forceps, scalpels and catheters so modern-looking and delicate. Medical centres grew up in many parts of the Hellenic world, often round shrines of Aesculapius, which added the quiet sanctity of temples to the cleanliness and efficiency of hospitals. Such were the shrines in Epidaurus and Cos.

In Galen, who flourished in the reign of Marcus Aurelius, the Roman Empire has one great name to contribute to the history of Greek medicine. Galen struck out no new particular branch of his own, but collected all the good material he could lay his hands on and systematized it. He was the last great doctor and down to the end of the Middle Ages he was the Aristotle of medicine.

LITERATURE

Letters played a very much smaller part in the world of Rome than they do in the world of today. There were no popular novels, no popular press, nothing of the mass of cheap periodicals such as provides the leisure reading of the millions today. Education was for the few and printing had not been born. Between the books read today by the student of Latin and the everyday speech of the Roman masses stretched a wider gulf than exists between highbrow and lowbrow reading today. Literature in the small democratic State of Athens had been the affair of all citizens; the greatest drama of the ancient world—the tragedies of Aeschylus,

Sophocles and Euripides, the comedies of Aristophanes and Menander and their many compeers—was produced for the people; the people became skilled to appraise the rhetoric of their politicians; Homer was a Bible. For in Greece literature developed naturally as the expression of a society; the lays of heroes which are the epic come first as the expression of the heroic age, a sort of community literature; then follows the age of lyric as men came to assert their individualism; and after that the drama was born, and tragedy was the reincarnation of heroic myth in the new world of individual vision, serving the new communal vigour of the small city-state. Only after these three stages were evolved did the age of criticism and pedantry and academic embroidery begin. But in Rome literature did not develop in the natural order; too much of it remained self-conscious where it should have been spontaneous. Here and there it reached great peaks, but in almost all its branches its writers were acutely aware of their inferiority to the Greek writers on whom they modelled themselves, and over-anxious to conform to correct Greek critical standards. "I pipe but as the linnet sings; I sing because I must," is the true poet's claim; only one Roman poet could with any justice make it. Too often the Roman poet was more concerned with being the Roman Homer or the Roman Hesiod or the Roman Callimachus; it is hard to write a good letter when you have a copy of *The Complete Letter Writer* open in front of you. With the whole brilliant panorama of Greek literature complete before its bewildered but admiring eyes, and possessed of an infinite capacity for borrowing good things, the Roman mind developed its literary expression in a topsy-turvy order. Instead of beginning with epic and working through ballad and lyric to drama, which is the natural order of progression evidenced by many cultures, it began with drama, and its epic was the last mode to come to full fruition. So we say, looking back over the ancient field, in which the Greek everywhere holds primacy; yet Rome has a way, in the literary no less than in other spheres, of confounding its critics. Miracle though it may be, with all its fits and starts and foregone failures, Roman literature has much to offer of abiding worth. Virgil, Cicero, Lucretius, Livy are constellations as surely set in the cosmos of letters as are Homer, Demosthenes, Plato and Thucydides.

Roman literature began almost by accident. Livius Andronicus (whom we have mentioned in the section on the Theatre), growing tired of the Twelve Tables as a text-book for his pupils, hit upon the happy idea of translating the Odyssey into Latin. The result was somewhat crude, but it had life, and a start had been made. That was in 240 B.C. He went on to adapt Greek dramas into Latin dress. By the end of the next century something like a Latin school of drama had been born and died—Naevius, Pacuvius, Accius, Caecilius Statius, Plautus and Terence; only the works of the last two have lived. Epic, too, had come into being: Ennius had written the *Annals of Rome* and Naevius a *Second Punic War*. Further histories, including several on the Punic Wars, didactic treatises (including works on law and Cato's classic *On Agriculture*) had seen the light of day, and a uniquely Roman type of literature, Satire, had asserted itself in the miscellanies of Ennius and the ferocious political invectives of Lucilius. Lastly, there were a few collections of speeches, notably those of Appius Claudius and Cato the censor, that might rank as literature. In all this there is a certain pedestrian, utilitarian quality characteristic of things Roman. Roman writing was either, as in much of its drama, a function of certain state ceremonials, or directed to some practical end. For the literature of the spirit the gently-nurtured had to cultivate Greek, which by the middle of the second century B.C. was established as an essential of the higher education.

The age of Caesar saw a marked advance in the range and quality of literature. Pure poetic activity, after a half-century or more of experiment in lyric and epigram on the lines of late Greek Alexandrian models, culminated in the brilliant and passionate intensity of Catullus, who died in the year in which Caesar invaded Britain for the second time. Caesar himself left to posterity a reputation as an orator of pith and force and, more concretely, the note-books in which he traced the course of his Gallic wars in order to justify to his contemporaries campaigns which he had undertaken without the sanction of the home government. These books, traditionally the terror of the modern schoolboy set to grapple with the first stages of a course in Latin, are a monument of clean-cut and vigorous narrative as hard and dynamic as Caesar's own face as we see it in the portrait-busts. He wrote a similar history of his Civil Wars and, besides these monumental works, a number of other minor works of a fine and versatile scholarship. To the same age belongs the great poem of Lucretius *On the Nature of Things* (see p. 146), an inspired exposition of Epicurean philosophy and science written with the fervour of a prophet; the works on law by Servius Sulpicius and Mucius Scaevola; the encyclopaedic lore of Varro; and, more significant for the future than all, the speeches and philosophic writings of Cicero. In Cicero Latin prose reached its peak; from its birth it had been a thing of force and weight, a fitting instrument of a nation of soldiers and men of action; now it acquired elasticity and poise. Setting himself to become the Roman Demosthenes, Cicero had achieved his aim; he lived and moved in the thick of political strife and, like Demosthenes, lost his life in the course of it. In his aim to be the Roman Plato he was less successful, for he was an appreciator of philosophers not a philosopher himself; but his treatises *On Duty, On the Limits of Good and Evil,* on political theory and other philosophical topics were valuable surveys cherished by posterity. He was a prolific letter-writer, too, and not the least of posterity's debts to him is for the full and many-sided picture of himself and of his age which his letters reveal. As Quintilian observed a century later, Cicero is no longer the name of a man, it is the name of eloquence itself. And over a thousand years later, when Europe after the long sleep of the Dark and Middle Ages turned again to the lost culture of the Greeks, it was the Latin of Cicero which the educators, the humanists, revived as the fit vehicle of Greek thought. Thus it was Cicero who provided the bridge between the ancient wisdom and the modern age which it fertilized. Last of the literary figures of the last century of the Republic we must mention Sallust, a historian in a new vein of thoughtful and painstaking scepticism, who has left us two pregnant monographs on the war with Jugurtha and on the Catilinarian conspiracy, heralding the new terse Latinity of the Silver Age; and the less significant Cornelius Nepos, who wrote a number of biographies of old-time celebrities in a thin and simple style with a moralizing intent.

The age of Augustus produced in Virgil, Horace and Ovid the three most famous poets in the history of Latin literature and in Livy Rome's most celebrated historian. In this age literary talent was, by avowed policy, harnessed to the task of propaganda, of proclaiming both the greatness of Rome and its culmination in the new régime of the Principate. The recognition of this fact need not, however, detract from the appreciation of this literature's quality; the poet who is paid to sing does not automatically forfeit inspiration, and the Augustan writers were sincere believers in the Augustan age. It is an illuminating reflection that, of the three poets just mentioned, the two who wrote in the service of the government produced works of imperishable greatness, while Ovid, who refused such compliance and frittered his talent on trivial themes, has achieved a dubious immortality as a flawless and facile versifier. Virgil is the crowning glory of the age, as indeed of the whole course of Roman letters. His *Eclogues*, short pastoral sketches of country life for the most part as mannered and as elegantly derivative as a Wedgwood vase, are early works, whose occasional fire and depth and nobility of language promise greater things to come. In the *Georgics*, a poem in four books which is both a handbook for farmers and a piece of propaganda for the new Back to the Land movement, we see his genius rising to its full stature. In the *Aeneid* it comes to full flower. This noble epic of the legendary founding of Rome is a harmony of poetry and philosophy, coupled with a sense of history and a brooding profundity which sets it beside the *Iliad*, Dante's *Divine Comedy* and

Milton's *Paradise Lost* as one of the supreme documents of human destiny as revealed through the poet's eyes. Of Virgil's greatness Tennyson is as eloquent as in a short compass it is possible to be: " the golden phrase," " the majestic sadness," " the stateliest measure ever moulded by the lips of man " are all essential ingredients in this sublime poetry.

Of Horace it is easier to speak. Perfect craftsman though he was and living inspiration though his poetry has been, his genius is of a more comfortable quality. Where Virgil is a mystic and a prophet, Horace is a man among men, a warm eulogist of the good things of life, of wine and peace, of the modest home and cheerful fireside, of the gentle philosophy which consists largely in the sense of gratitude for good things received and falls just this side complacency. His greatest works are the four books of Odes on a variety of patriotic themes, in which he combined the melodious rhythms of the Greek lyricists and the sonorous dignity of Latin with consummate success. The secret of these odes is rather one of craftsmanship than of sensibility. They lack the depth and the young intensity of a Sappho or a Catullus; they reflect rather the poised and matured enthusiasms of middle age; the expression is that of the connoisseur, refined, calculated, lapidary. Yet Horace knows how to put his finger on the pulses of national, as of individual, emotion, and some of his odes on great Roman deeds of the past show the two magnificently fused. Horace has left us other works on satirical, moralizing and literary themes, showing a lively interest in men and manners and a critical sense, all couched in a style somewhat reminding us of Pope; but his true greatness is in the Odes.

Ovid has left us a great volume of verse of varying merit on various themes, pleasant rehashes of old· romantic love themes and legends, lascivious and mock-didactic treatises on the arts of courtship and love and a book of the stories clustering round the Roman calendar. In these writings he displayed a versatility, a gift for narrative, and a mastery of technique which has become a byword; as Virgil raised the hexameter verse to be the stateliest of human measures, so Ovid raised the Latin elegiac couplet to the exquisitely modulated vehicle for those intimate and contemplative poetic revelations which lie between the spontaneity of the lyric and the grandeur of epic. It is sad that, having perfected this delicate instrument, Ovid never made full use of it but spent it on second-class themes. Propertius, another elegiac writer of the time, though he lacked the Ovidian perfection of style, is greater, for he wrote from the heart. His love elegies are deeper and more passionate than those of Tibullus, another contemporary, whose graceful verse lacked the energy of Ovid though it had his smooth touch.

In 26 B.C., Livy began his great *History of Rome*, which told the story of Rome from the earliest times and ran to 142 books, of which some 35 survive. By modern standards he would not pass muster as a scientific historian; his art is more conspicuous than his skill; but he took pains to examine his sources and wrote with a comprehensive outlook and a large conception of his subject, the growth to greatness of the Roman people. He interpreted the spirit of Rome with compelling felicity and unfolded her story as a long and colourful pageant. His style is admirably flexible, now full and rich, now terse and incisive; his pictures are vivid, his

character-sketches rounded, his narrative of great eloquence and power. He did for Latin prose what the
Virgilian hexameter did for poetry.

In these writers and many others whose works have
not come down to us (Augustan drama, for instance, is
for us a closed book), Roman literature reached its
maturity. During the following centuries of the Empire
there was much to come, but the Augustan was the
Golden Age and the norm. Behind it lay the archaic
age of experiment in which Roman culture wrestled
with the angel of Greek to achieve self-expression and
self-respect; in front lay the sheltered calm of the
Principate, which gave leisure and breathing-space but
dimmed the vital spark. For literature is a plant which
thrives in freedom and in stress and languishes where
the atmosphere is too rigidly controlled. The monarch-
ic system of the Empire could not tolerate the free speech
and thought of turbulent republican days, and paid the
price in letters. There was no Cicero or Sallust, no
Milton or Euripides under the Empire; it was too
dangerous. Consequently, there are many names in
the history of literature in the Silver Age, but few
that are great. There were the historian Tacitus,
brilliant, rhetorical, embittered, wielder of a new
terse and trenchant prose, and the bitter and caustic
satirist Juvenal, free only in retrospect, the epigram-
matist Martial, Quintilian the writer on education,
Lucan who wrote an epic on the campaign of Pharsalus,
Petronius who produced the first Latin novel, the
younger Seneca who perfected the philosophic epistle
and wrote many tragedies which we would gladly
exchange for others. There were Pliny the Elder, who
amassed an encyclopaedia of miscellaneous knowledge

which in quality is little better than a giant Ripley, and his nephew, Pliny the Younger, a diligent letter-writer who set himself to emulate Cicero. There was a mass of pretentious and tedious epic and tragedies not proof against the ravages of mice and dust and contemporary neglect. From the second century to the fourth Latin literature flows on in a wide but shallow stream of mediocrity (Suetonius, Aulus Gellius, Fronto, Apuleius cannot be ranked among the great names in the world of letters) until with the triumph of Christianity a new force surges in to produce, among others, Tertullian, an impassioned Puritan lashing with brilliant rhetoric, irony and invective the vices of pagan Rome; the scholarly Jerome; Prudentius, the only considerable poet of Latin Christendom and forerunner of the Latin poetry of the Middle Ages; and the great Augustine of Hippo, author of the world-famous *Confessions* and *The City of God*.

ARCHITECTURE AND FINE ARTS

Among a practically-minded people architecture, the most useful of arts, was likely to dwarf the arts of pure expression. As wealth increased and Romans became increasingly conscious of the luxuries of the Hellenistic world, painting and sculpture came to play their part in the apparatus of Roman culture; but painting never found Roman roots, and sculpture took on Roman character only in the semi-utilitarian provinces of the portrait-bust and the architectural relief. But building such things as houses, temples, public monuments, baths, aqueducts, bridges, triumphal arches was an activity congenial to the Roman mind.

Building materials in early times were simple and

economically used. Houses were of sun-dried brick, timber and plaster. The commonest stone was the soft volcanic tufa, ready to hand on the western coast. In time, better and harder stone was obtained from the hill-country of central Italy, notably travertine, a durable cream limestone from the region round Tivoli, which came into common use in the last century B.C. and under the Empire. Marble, imported from Greek sources, began to come in from the middle of the second century B.C., as Rome sought to emulate the magnificent buildings of the Greek world now opening up before its eyes. It was Augustus's boast that he had found in Rome a city of brick and had left it a city of marble. The lands of the Levant, indeed, had to offer a wonderful variety of this beautiful stone; the fine-grained white marble of Pentelicus in Attica, which took on a warm golden tinge in weathering, and the pure lustrous white of Paros, to mention but two of the many marbles from Greece; beside these the famous Italian marble from Carrara was too dull and close-textured to compete in beauty. To these white stones Roman taste often preferred the variegated—the Numidian (yellow veined with rose), the Phrygian (white streaked with purple), the green and white from Carystus in Euboea. Similarly prized were the red granites and the red and green porphyries imported from Egypt.

By the second century B.C. the early buildings of square, unmortared blocks were giving place to concrete buildings faced with small stone blocks gradually becoming more regular in form and size, and by the time of the Empire brick and concrete were the usual materials for buildings not meant for display. This invention of concrete was an important factor in the development of Roman architecture and served the evolution of the arch, the vault and the dome, which became the characteristic features of its culminating phase.

The first phase is that represented by the Greek temple, all straight lines, the architecture of the column and architrave. For such building the three Greek orders were all used (the Doric with the plain, square capital; the Ionic, usually fluted, with the ram's horns spirals on the capital; the Corinthian, in which the deep leaf-carved capital is merged as an ornamental finish into the top of the shaft) and, earlier, the old Tuscan order, a plain unfluted column, of Etruscan origin, similar to the Doric. For temples the architecture of column and architrave remained the norm, elaborated in time by all the intricacies of moulding and carving on frieze and metope that could be devised within the classic framework. But Rome had her variants on the old austere rectangular models. Sometimes the columns were on three sides only; sometimes circular temples were built with columns all round, such as the temple of Vesta in the Forum. A striking difference between the classic Greek temple and most Roman temples of the mature period was the raising of the building high above ground-level, so that it was approached by a high flight of steps. The Greek temple was built on a shallow platform involving no more than two or three steps; the Hellenistic and Roman extension of this feature survives in many public buildings of today.

An extension of column architecture is seen in the development of the Hellenistic colonnade, used to border public places and important thoroughfares, and of the colonnaded court. The colonnade became the stamp of

Roman urbanization and, as such, is seen even on the remote fringes of Empire—at Palmyra in the Syrian desert and at Timgad in Africa. Roman, too, was the use of the columns, whether grouped or single, for purely ornamental purposes in public monuments. Such are the great columns of Trajan and Marcus Aurelius, wrapped in their spirals of sculptured reliefs, still to be seen in Rome.

But the great Roman contribution to architecture was that of the pier and the arch, which was first used for the construction of bridges and aqueducts. Extended to other architecture, it produced the arcade and the pilaster (a flattened, functionless version of the pillar applied to the pier to relieve its bareness and to convey the impression of the column and architrave construction). The arcade made for strength, and arcades could be superimposed one on another to produce complex constructions of great size and dignity. Such was the Colosseum (built by Vespasian and his son Titus), which is an object-lesson in the development of Roman architecture. Here are the three classic Greek orders used in the right chronological order, Ionic on Doric, Corinthian on Ionic, to mask the piers of a triple-storied arcading, the whole in perfect proportion, shaped into the perfect dynamic round of an amphitheatre, seating 50,000 spectators. In the phase of the pier and the arch the development of the triumphal arch corresponds to that of the column-monument in the earlier phase. Triumphal arches in varying degrees of elaboration and applied decoration, commonly enriched with sculptured reliefs and inscriptions on the high entablature above the arch, are found scattered in profusion in the provinces of the Western Empire. Famous examples are the

14

arches of Septimius Severus (in the Forum just below the Capitol at Rome) and of Titus (near the Colosseum, sculptured with scenes of the destruction of Jerusalem).

The culminating phase in Roman architecture was that of the vault and the dome, made possible by the invention of concrete. Once the art of constructing the barrel vault had been mastered, the building of intersecting, groined vaults (which distributed the weight and stress of the superstructure to key points) and the dome naturally followed. On this plan were built the large bath-halls of the imperial age. A striking contrast between this type of architecture and that of the earlier phase was that here it was the interior of the building that received ornamentation; the outside remained relatively bare. In interiors decorative arches and columns multiplied and much use was made of panels on the underside of vaults and domes with ornament in paint, gilt and stucco. Domes were made of converging vaults, as in the octagonal-vaulted dome of the great Baths of Caracalla, or they might, like the Pantheon, rest simply on circular walls.

Fortifications, the building of city walls such as those of Aurelian (substantial remains of which can be seen at Rome), bridges, aqueducts, these were the commonest and most typical products of the practical genius of Roman architecture. Thinking of the spectacular buildings which figure most prominently among the illustrations of the text-books, of the Colosseum and the Pantheon, of the academic temples, we must not forget the great wall which in Hadrian's time was driven across Britain from Tyne to Solway, or the noble bridges of Roman Spain, or the strong praetorium of Lambaesis in Africa. For in such structures, planned without regard to mere looks and without an uneasy deference to Greek canons, Rome achieved architecture strong, solid and unpretentious, yet possessed of a dignity all its own.

Roman sculpture, like other arts, was largely ruled· by outside influences. The sculpture of the early republican period was governed by Etruscan models and shows, in the cult images of terra-cotta and bronze, the vigorous realism which characterized Etruscan representational art. Similarly Etruscan in feeling are the decorative terra-cotta plaques and bas-reliefs. From the third century B.C. the Etruscan influence waned before the ever-increasing influx of Greek inspirations: and sculpture of a nobler and more imposing cast began to develop. The early Empire brought an age of sculptural activity. Elaborate high-reliefs in marble became common; a noble example is the panels of the Ara Pacis, with its stately grouped scenes of Roman civic life. Fine reliefs are found on most of the triumphal monuments: Trajan's column, built to commemorate his Dacian wars, contains in its broad spiral of relief some 150 scenes of animated military activity, executed with vigour in realistic detail. Ornamentation in relief became a favourite device for relieving plain surfaces on tombs and altars; to this end luxuriant and conventionalized plant-forms were much used and often produced work of rich and fluid beauty.

Portrait-sculpture was an art in which the Roman craftsman, with his realist *penchant*, excelled. It had its roots in the Roman's strong family-sense and in the veneration of ancestors. Materially it began with the practice of making death-masks (by pouring melted wax over the dead man's face) which the Romans borrowed from the Etruscans. These masks were preserved, set up in the house and carried in funeral processions, and so acquired an artistic permanence. As Greek marble and Greek sculpture came to influence Roman ideas, portrait-busts became increasingly common and under the early Empire reached a high pitch of excellence. These busts are not concerned with the ideal types of Greek sculpture; they are faithful renderings of individuals, with little attempt to gloss over or idealize. Characterized by painstaking attention to detail, they reflect minutely the vagaries of contemporary fashion. Looking at the lines of busts in the museums we can in a moment distinguish the honeycomb coiffure affected by society ladies of the age of Domitian from the tight, stylized curls of a generation later and still more certainly from the simpler styles of the middle of the second century. The full and ordered array of portrait-busts of the Empire provides a complete commentary on the story of Roman society. So, too, does the range of Roman coinage, not the least impressive chapter of Roman art. The coins of the Empire show a similar technical excellence, rising to a peak at the end of the second century A.D., and thence declining. The fleshy handsomeness of Nero, the hardheaded bourgeois ugliness of Vespasian, the aristocratic haggardness of Nerva, the haughty Domitian, the dilettante Hadrian, the Olympian beauty of Antoninus are stamped for perpetuity in the bronze and gold of their coinages. A similar excellence is to be seen in the cameos and gem-engravings of the Empire.

Few specimens of Roman painting survive beyond those contained in the mural decorations of Pompeii and some other Italian sites. Mural decorations in painting developed through four well-defined phases. In the first phase the art was of a low order; the decorator divided the wall-surface into panels before the plaster was dry and painted them to imitate the rich marble interiors of Hellenistic palaces. In the second or "architectural" phase, the classic decorative style of the age of Augustus, the wall-surfaces are more realistically and thoroughly divided by columns with full capitals and entablatures painted on the flat and the panels are fitted with scenic pictures in perspective, vistas of houses and terraced gardens and country shrines. In the third, the "ornate," style the painted architectural constructions no longer aim at producing illusory effects, but develop into fanciful, luxuriant, delicate patternings of a purely decorative character, while inside the panels figures predominate. The fourth, commonly called the "intricate," style is an extension of the second, carrying architectural forms into a complex, fantastic multiplicity with the elegance and the artificiality of the baroque. The panel-pictures of room-walls range from allegorical subjects and scenes from legends to mere filling of conventional scrolls and wreaths. In purely decorative filling floral and architectural motifs play a conspicuous part; they also show a liking for motifs taken from natural life, birds and beasts and fruit. It is clear from ancient writers that easel-pictures were also produced, though this department never assumed in the ancient world the importance it has enjoyed in the modern. Ancient painting of the human figure reached a high degree of merit and shows a mastery of the use of light and shade and a good handling of perspective. Mosaic craft, of which we have spoken in an earlier chapter, followed closely the subjects of painting, and reached a similar excellence.

Other arts there were which we can do no more than mention: the art of the letter-engraver in stone, which went to make Roman lettering, with its austere beauty, a living factor in our world of art; the arts of pottery-making, glass, metal-work, of landscape-gardener and jeweller. Music in the ancient world never had the independent status which it has enjoyed since the Renaissance; it was a handmaid of drama, lyric poetry and religious ceremonial. Here, too, Rome preserved what the Greek world had given her. If Roman originality is dwarfed by comparison with the priceless inventions of the Greek genius, we must not write off the Romans as an inartistic people. They garnered the noble arts of the Mediterranean world with possessive care and, though the hand of the *nouveau riche* often showed, made their houses and towns things of dignity and beauty. Thanks to this discernment and devotion much of the ancient arts endured through the Dark Ages to enrich the world we know.

CHAPTER X

GREATER ROME

Fecisti patriam diversis gentibus unam . . .
urbem fecisti quod prius orbis erat.—RUTILIUS.

"You have made the earth's diversity into one great country; you have made a city what was once a world."

"IT was a god who gave us this peace," cries the countryman in Virgil; and if it was an exaggeration it was pardonable. Augustus not only adjusted the disharmonics of the body politic of Rome, not only gave peace after the desolation of the civil wars; he laid the foundations of a continuing calm. In this new calm men opened the eyes which they had shut against the horrors of the last century and saw a new world with receding horizons. Livy, starting his history before the new age had dawned, might write that he found spiritual refuge in the story of the old days; but the poets looked forward. "God's in his Heaven; all's right with the world" is Horace's theme in the beginning of a well-known ode, and Virgil's Fourth *Eclogue*, though its immediate occasion was an event which proved of small consequence, reads like the thirty-fifth chapter of Isaiah.

"On thee, child, first shall Earth pour the gifts of childhood, untilled, the wandering vine-tendril and the foxglove, marsh-lily and the smiling acanthus. Unherded shall the goats bring home full udders, nor shall lions fright the herd. Unbidden shall the ground you lie on burgeon with sweet flowers. The snake shall die and the treacherous poison-plant shall die; everywhere shall blossom the fragrant herb. Then once you shall grow to read the lays of the heroes and of your father's great deeds and to know the shape of true goodness, slowly the field shall grow gold with the tender ear, and on the wild briar shall the dark grape hang and the tough oak shall drip the dew of honey . . ."

The parallel is striking. In that vision lies more than a hint of the true greatness of the Roman Empire, of the power which gave freedom from enemies without and within; which drew firm boundaries on the edges and policed them with armies; which swept away pirates and brigands from seas and roads; which made roads, good roads, and kept them in repair and furnished them with milestones and sign-pillars; which mapped the Mediterranean world into a self-conscious and habitable whole. Travel became safe and trade grew and flourished in this new, well-articulated realm, as it had never flourished before.

COMMUNICATIONS

There were two ways of getting about the Mediterranean world, by sea and by land. The Greeks were the great sailors; where they could, the Romans preferred to march. So, when we turn to consider Roman travel and communications, roads must come first.

Roman roads (there is something especially symbolic, almost proverbial about the phrase, and certainly no article of the Roman civilization is so much mentioned in common speech) have two outstanding characteristics: their directness and their solidity. They may not always have been very scientifically constructed; very

often as we watch a Roman road cleaving straight
through a variegated landscape, we feel that a better
road-engineer would have consulted contours to better
effect and have been more economical of material and
effort; but they were masterful. They suggest, as Mr.
Hilaire Belloc has written, " swiftness and certitude of
aim and a sort of eager determination which we are
slow to connect with government, but which certainly
underlay the triumph of this people." And they did
what they were meant to do, which was to convey
legions from one point to another as rapidly as was
possible. For they were primarily military roads, an
essential part of Rome's apparatus for controlling new
areas which came under her sway. The Appian Way,
for instance, was built to strengthen the Roman hold
on Campania. The Fosse Way in England is a particularly good example of the point. Until recently
scholars were at a loss to explain its purpose; as has been
said, it seems to run from nowhere in particular to
nowhere else in particular. It has now been shown that
it was meant as a frontier demarcation at the end of the
first phase of the Roman conquest of Britain. All to
the south-east of this line was Roman; on the other side
stretched the region still to be conquered; between the
two great tracts ran the unerring line of the Roman
road, not only a dividing line but a highway along
which troops could be rushed to any point which
threatened danger. Since, then, Roman roads were
primarily strategical, they were systematic, built in
careful inter-communication.

With their directness goes their solidity. The builder
of a Roman road did not shrink from cutting through
rock which his modern counterpart would go round or

from carrying his communications on long viaducts straight across valleys where we should go gently down and up. And when he had got his line he built a road that would last. His highways were dug out three and four feet deep and compounded of successive layers of gravel and stone and cement, the whole paved with large blocks of stone closely fitted together and carefully cambered to carry off the rain. They were of no great width, for the most part fifteen feet wide at most; but some of them had subsidiary roads beside them for local traffic and sometimes sidewalks for pedestrians. Along them were set milestones marking the distance from Rome or other important towns. Many of these survive, and some of the great bridges and viaducts over which great trunk roads passed are still standing strong after nearly 2,000 years. The Pont du Gard, near Nîmes, is a striking specimen of the massive skill with which Roman communications might be forged.

Such were the roads along which Roman legions marched, often with astonishing speed (we may remember Suetonius Paulinus's great march down the Watling Street—the London–Holyhead road—A5—when Boudicca rose in A.D. 61); along which the couriers of the imperial post might with ease cover 100 miles a day (there is the record of the messenger who brought the news of Nero's death in A.D. 68 to Galba in Spain, 332 miles in thirty-six hours) and the ordinary traveller average a round fifty.

Travel by Land

It is with the ordinary traveller that we are for the moment concerned. How would he travel? Your poor man might ride his donkey or mule or even walk;

officials and young gentlemen we should find with their
attendants on horseback; but the important man and
the comfortably-well-off traveller would ride in a litter
or, for a longer journey, in a carriage.

Litters were especially common in Rome, where the
narrow streets and the density of the traffic made it
necessary for the authorities to prohibit wheeled traffic
during the daytime. The litter was a couch with a
canopy and side-curtains slung on poles which were
shouldered, according to the size of the litter or the
wealth of the owner, by two, six or eight slaves. Sometimes a sedan-chair was used. Carriages were of various
kinds. For fast travelling there were light gigs (*cisia* or
esseda), two-wheeled and drawn by a couple of mules
or, better, of fast Gallic ponies. The *carpentum* was a
stronger form of two-wheeled chaise. These were the
ancient equivalent of taxicabs and could readily be
hired at the gates of towns, nor were taximeters (there
was a device called the hodometer invented by Hero of
Alexandria) unknown. For heavier travelling, in the
place of the coach or the family limousine, was the
raeda, a large four-wheeled carriage, which for a wealthy
man might be as cushioned and elegant as the travelling-
coach of a rich nobleman of the eighteenth century.

Roadside inns were frequent, but more taverns than
hotels, and catered only for the humble traveller. As
in later times, they were known by signs—*Ad Gallum*,
" At the Sign of the Cock," *Ad Rotam*, " The Wheel."
Food and wine were cheap at such hostelries (witness
the Good Samaritan's modest two " pence "), but the
company might be very mixed and the traveller who
was not prepared to risk a noisy evening and a none too
clean bed would take pains, if possible, to stay with

friends at various stages of his way. Rich men, like Cicero, with their villas and many acquaintances, might never be at a loss for a night's comfortable lodging on a journey in Italy. But it is clear from Horace's semi-humorous account of his journey with Maecenas from Rome to Brundisium that, on the whole, one did not travel for pleasure.

SEA TRAVEL

Sea travel was rather more precarious. There was little organization in the way of passenger services and private sea-voyaging was largely opportunist. An experienced traveller would have little difficulty in picking up passages stage by stage in merchantmen and coasting vessels, very much after the fashion of " lorry-hopping " in our times, but he would not have to put too much reliance on times or to look for travel by sea earlier than the beginning of March or later than mid-November. We may recall the stages by which the Roman authorities had to convey an important political prisoner from Jerusalem to Rome in the year 58–9 for trial before an imperial court:

> " And embarking in a ship of Adramyttium, which was about to sail unto the places on the coast of Asia, we put to sea . . . and the next day we touched at Sidon . . . and putting to sea from thence, we sailed under the lee of Cyprus, because the winds were contrary. And when we had sailed across the sea which is off Cilicia and Pamphylia, we came to Myra, a city of Lycia. And there the centurion found a ship of Alexandria sailing for Italy ; and he put us therein. . . ."

A good-sized merchantman, say a grain-ship, in which a traveller might look to find a passage from Alexandria to Puteoli, would be a vessel of 400–500 tons. It would be rigged with a large mainsail on a great central mast, with small foresail and topsail; its length would be about 150 feet, 30 perhaps in the beam. In the larger ships there would be tolerable cabin-space, though of limited appointment. Such, no doubt, was the sort of ship in which Saint Paul got nearly as far as Malta.

Under the Republic travel had not been too safe. Brigands on the roads and pirates on the seas were part of the normal hazards of travelling until the end of the last century B.C. and the establishment of a strong central government. Much of the spade-work in making the world safe for the traveller was done by Pompey, who swept the Mediterranean clear of pirates in a few months in 67 B.C., and by Julius Caesar, but it was not till the age of Augustus that real safety was assured.

The World of the Empire

Let us look at this world of Rome as it was in the Augustan age. Starting from the Forum, where stands the Golden Milestone, in which all the roads that lead to Rome are tied together, as it were, in a central knot, we leave Rome through the Capena gate by the via Appia, the Great South Road. Past the villas and tombs which fringe it for a few miles out, we pursue it over the Alban hills, down the Pomptine flats and so along the coast till we turn inland to Capua. Here we leave on our left the via Popilia, the highroad for the toe of Italy and Sicily, and continue on the via Appia up through the vineyards of the hill-country to Beneventum, Venusia, to the port of Tarentum and thence through the Calabrian pastures to the bustling crowded harbour-town of Brindisi. The road, except for the last section and a bad patch over the Pomptine marshes, was a good one, and it has taken ten days.

Here we take ship for Greece. If we liked we could book a passage straight across the Adriatic to Apollonia and from there, travelling due east along the via Egnatia, reach Byzantium (Constantinople) in twenty days. But we are bound elsewhere. We sail down the Epirot coast, gazing at the coastal hills. Though the deep, variegated channels and gullies pit them with all shades of purple and brown in the hot summer sun, they look uninviting and desolate, a home for pirates. But these are gone now. We run under the lee of Corcyra, inside Leucas, past Odysseus's' Ithaca, very small and quiet, past the new monuments of the Victory Town erected to commemorate the great battle of Actium and the first place to show any life on any land we have so far passed, and put into the Gulf of Corinth. We call at Patrae, a busy port to which a Roman colony has recently given new life. For it is important. It exports the fine linens woven from the flax of Elis and the textiles of Sparta. We sail along the northern coast of the Corinthian gulf watching till we see Itea, the port of Delphi. Perhaps we may pause here to visit the famous shrine of Apollo: a long laborious climb on a winding uphill road; no Roman road this, but an affair of thick white dust and loose stones, as we mount past the rich oliveyards of the Crisean plain, which soon are spread below us like a sea, to the cleft deep in the tall strange mountains, frightening for all the sunlight.

It will be tempting to linger at this ancient seat of Greek religion, to meditate on the symbols of a culture which led in due time to the flowering of a civilization which had fallen at the feet of Rome. But what did

Greece mean to Rome ? A land from which vitality, as the world counts vitality, had gone; a land poor compared with Italy. Yet there were still the vineyards and the oliveyards whose olives were sweeter than those from Spain; breeds of horses and asses which Rome was glad to make use of; fine linens from Elis, the best honey in the world from Hymettus in Attica, the best purple-dyes from Cythera, sundry other dyes and perfumes and, above all, the marble. And in the cities were the makers of the works of art which the wealthy Roman coveted for his villas, statues and statuettes in marble and bronze, exquisite lamps and vases. Nor must we forget the human export; the facile and quick-witted Greek was as proverbial for his migratory flair in the ancient world as is the Scot in the modern, and in-variably as efficient.

From Delphi we resume the journey to Corinth, the great port which stands on its isthmus between the two seas and controls the trade of both. Through it mer-chants journey not only from north and south but also from east to west. There is no Corinth canal yet, but it is better to pay the dues to have your ship dragged on the rollers across the isthmus than to risk a doubtful passage round Cape Malea. From Corinth run roads north to Megara, Athens and Boeotia, west to Sicyon, Phlius and Patrae, south-east to Epidaurus and Troezen, to Argos and thence to the south. They are poor roads; for there is not much traffic in the Peloponnese and sea-borne carriage is easier.

From Corinth we proceed once more by sea round Salamis, to the Peiraeus and Athens. Corinth is still a busy port, handling for export olive-oil and wine, marble, horses and asses from the Argive plain, textiles, dyes and perfumes and the mass-produced works of art we have mentioned. But the Peiraeus is only a shadow of its former self, though it still exports the famous Attic olive-oil, Hymettan honey and the marble of Pentelicus. The famous Laurion silver-mines, which meant so much to fifth-century Athens, are exhausted. Athens is still revered as a great university-town, a little eclipsed by Alexandria, but Roman students still attend its schools of rhetoric and philosophy and the Acropolis and its ancient monuments are still wonders of the world.

To the north there is Thessaly, noted for its corn-crops and, as ever, for its horses; Macedon, sending excellent timber from its well-wooded mountains; and Thrace, a hardy land which breeds good soldiers and stout slaves, where gold is still to be found in Mount Pangaeus.

But there is no time to wander to the north or to linger in the pleasant islands of the Aegean. We thread our way through the Cyclades, past Andros and Delos (Apollo's birthplace and other home, once a great centre of the slave-trade), to Cos, where the cool temple-hospital is one of the shrines of Greek medicine, and to Rhodes, that sophisticated island between East and West where Julius Caesar learnt his rhetoric and where Tiberius is to retire to his astrology when tired of the political race. From Rhodes the Etesian winds carry us south in three days to Alexandria, the most brilliant city in the world.

Our first impression of Alexandria is of its complexity: the great lighthouse, the fine harbours, on the west side of the Nile delta, the many intersecting waterways linking up all the channels of the delta itself, all busy day and night with shipping of all sizes, cargo-boats and pleasure-boats, and brimming with life. Here from the easternmost arm of the Nile is a canal, 150 feet wide, leading to Arsinoe on the Red Sea. For Alexandria is the hub of Eastern Mediterranean trade. To it by caravan routes overland come the ivory of Africa, the spices of Arabia, the cottons and silks from India and the East, the pearls of the Persian Gulf. Up the Red Sea from the port of Myos Hormos come the beautiful red granite blocks, the black basalt and the green and red porphyry from the mountains east of the Nile and, from the region of Berenice, amethysts and beryls. From far in the south come the gold and iron of Ethiopia. On the western side are the caravan routes leading to Cyrene, rich in cereals, oil and wine, sheep and horses and the valuable silphium plant, and to the Roman province of Africa (Tripoli).

And what of Egypt herself? Here is a country so rich that it is not governed like an ordinary province, but under a prefect specially appointed by the Emperor, and no senator can set foot in it on pain of death. For here was the granary of the Roman world, so vital that Emperors were specially concerned to keep the irrigation system in good order and to do all they could to facilitate the convoy of the huge grain cargoes to Italy. The fertility of the Nile valley was phenomenal; there was not only wheat but barley, millet, spelt and sesame; flax, beans, lentils, cucumbers, melons; in some districts the olive and the vine and, in the south, the date-palm; in the orchards many fruits—pomegranate, fig, peach and cherry. The great exports were corn, dates and the papyrus plant on which the world depended for its paper (to which the plant has given its name); but there was much else: linens and delicate

15

glass, drugs, cosmetics, certain kinds of salt fish, jewelry and perfumes. Alexandria itself was no mere middle-man. She had workshops in which the raw materials of the East (silks, cottons, hides, ivory, jewels) were transformed into articles ready for the Bond Streets of the Roman world.

It is not surprising to find the population of Alexandria as variegated as its commerce and crafts. Egyptians, Greeks, Jews, Persians, Arabs, westerners and orientals (we can do worse than refer to the catalogue in *Acts*, chapter 2), all are here. There were riotings in some of the humbler quarters of the city at times, for life in such a complex of peoples where trade rivalry was so keen could not be invariably peaceful. There still survives a stern letter from the Emperor Claudius of the year A.D. 41, addressed to the people of Alexandria at large, in which he writes: " If you will not cease from this pestilential spite against each other I shall be compelled to show you what a humane ruler becomes when moved to righteous anger." The special reference is to the old feud between Greeks and Jews.

But trade is not the whole picture. Alexandria was also the leading university of the world, a Venice, a Paris and an Oxford rolled into one. Here was the centre of all learning. Here was the home of mathe-matics and the birthplace of philology. At Alexandria Ptolemy II had founded the original Museum, the pro-totype of the countless museums of the world, the great institute where, under the patronage of the enlightened dynasty of the Ptolemies, scholars and scientists lived, researched and taught at the expense of the State. With this central college went the two great libraries in which the whole field of world literature was collected,

catalogued and edited. It was Aristotle, at one time
the tutor of Alexander the Great (the founder of Alexandria), who had founded the scientific method of
research based on the collection and analysis of data,
and his method was the inspiration of the institutes of
Alexandria. It was inevitable that such an atmosphere
with such facilities should draw to it representatives of
all the known branches of science and that they should
flourish there. And if literature in such a milieu became
too pedantic and meticulous an affair to produce any
really vital result, it is equally true that, without the
labours of its Alexandrian pioneers, we should not have
modern science as we know it today.

And Alexandria was a beautiful city. Around its
skirts might cling all the meanness of harbour riff-raff,
but in the midst was a spacious city, with great squares
and broad avenues, shady colonnades and majestic
buildings, a city which had been planned for a greatness
which it had achieved. Pleasures and entertainment
abounded there; a famous second-century moralist
abuses the Alexandrians for their devotion to the theatre
and the games. As it enjoyed the amenities, so it
harboured the abuses which must spring up in any great
sophisticated metropolis. And it is no wonder that an
old-fashioned Roman, thinking of Cleopatra and the
influence she had had on the lives of Julius Caesar and
Mark Antony and on the course of Roman history itself,
and suspicious of all things in the Eastern half of his
world, should eye the great city askance.

There is no time to follow the trade-routes to the
Persian Gulf and the East, tempting though they are.
We know that by the end of the first century the sailors
of the West had found out the secret of the monsoon and

could sail straight to the mouth of the Indus. A regular trade sprang up between India and the Mediterranean. Nor did it stop there. There were not lacking adventurers to push even farther, past Ceylon to the Malay peninsula and to the Chinese emporia. Overland, too, a regular traffic with China came into being during the course of the century, greatly facilitated by the strong rule of the Han dynasty in China and the development of Chinese control over the Tarim plateau. On the overland connections, however, there were difficulties with the kingdom of Parthia which prevented the land-routes from ever rivalling in importance the sea-routes through the Indian Ocean. (We find a Chinese agent, one Kan-Ying, having an interview in the year A.D. 97 with the governor of Syria; and by 166 we hear of Greek traders at the court of the Emperor Huan-ti at Loyang averring that they come from the Emperor "An-tun," who must be none other than M. Aurelius Antoninus in Chinese dress.) And in another direction there were traders boldly feeling their way down the East African coast to Zanzibar and the Mozambique bay.

But for us at the moment these are travellers' tales. Our path lies north up the famous coast-road through Palestine and Syria to the Euphrates, the connecting link between the two rich lands of Mesopotamia and Egypt. Until the coming of Augustus this thin coastal strip had been more a road for conquering armies, for the marchings and countermarchings of Egyptians and Assyrians, of Ptolemies and Seleucids, down to the time of Antony's departure on his ill-fated conquest of Parthia, than a land to live in. Rome has made it prosperous and an avenue for trade. It is interesting to read in the letters of T. E. Lawrence:

" It is such a comfort to know that the country was not like this in the time of our Lord. The Renaissance painters were right who drew him and his disciples feasting in a pillared hall or sunning themselves on marble staircases: everywhere one finds remains of splendid Roman roads and houses and public buildings, and Galilee was the most Romanized province of Palestine. Also the country was well-peopled and well-watered artificially. There were not 20 miles of thistles behind Capernaum! and on the way round the lake they did not come upon dirty dilapidated Bedouin tents, with the people calling to them to come and talk while miserable curs came snapping at their heels; Palestine was a decent country. . . ."

From Pelusium the road kept to the coast as far as Gaza, where the route to Petra in Arabia Petraea branched off to join the route which went from the eastern arm of the Red Sea to serve the regions over Jordan. The main coast-road went on up to Tyre and Sidon, to Beyrouth and Seleucia, the port of the great city of Antioch. At Tyre another route branched off to Damascus and across the desert to the legendary Palmyra and so to the Euphrates. These caravan cities throve and reached great wealth under the arm of Rome: Petra with its noble temples cut from the living rock; Jerash with its theatre; Palmyra, which established itself as a middleman between the rival Roman and Parthian Empires and in its neutrality acquired the power which three centuries later made possible the romantic caravan-empire of Zenobia and Vaballath. All became cities of beauty and distinction, as trade increased between the Persian Gulf, Egypt, Syria and Mesopotamia; and Dura, the point where the caravan-route reached the Euphrates, one time Parthian caravan-city and one time Roman fortress, has recently proved a second Pompeii in the wealth of materials which it has afforded archaeologists for the understanding of an age in which so many cultures were interfused.

On the desert-fringe Roman power became vaguer and, with a free Parthian empire on the other side of the Euphrates, Rome was careful to keep Syria well guarded. There were usually four legions quartered in Syria to safeguard the all-important coast-road to Egypt as well as Syria itself. For the province itself was second only to Egypt in economic importance. First came the textile industry of Tyre and Sidon, of Berytus and Byblos; linens and silks and garments dyed with the famous purple that was obtained by crushing the purple shell-fish dredged up on the Phoenician coast. Tyre had glass-works too as well as dye factories; and Syrian perfumes were famous throughout the world. The land, too, was rich in produce : the precious wine of Laodicea, the plums, dates, figs, all manner of pre-served fruits, for which Damascus and Jericho in particular were famous; precious stones and spices. There were rich balsam groves near Jericho, and a steady export of bitumen from the Dead Sea.

Antioch, the capital of Syria, was a wonderful city, not so magnificent as Alexandria perhaps in its spacious-ness and lay-out, but more prodigal in the arts of material pleasure, a trippers' Babylon. Here were to be found pleasure-gardens and boulevards lit by night and day, luxurious temples, courts and colonnades, and the costly houses of prosperous merchants who grew rich on the trade which passed through their country. There was one great avenue paved entirely in marble

blocks, the gift of Herod Agrippa of Judaea. The
people were made of soft stuff, thought the Romans
(and Syria was a notorious region for weakening the
morale of Roman garrisons), but they were glad to
import Syrian musicians, actors and dancers. " Syrian"
for a Roman satirist was a synonym for " dago "; it is
the Orontes, the river of Syria, which for him has
polluted the Tiber, the symbol of Rome pure and
undefiled.

Setting his face once more towards Rome the tourist
sails in a coasting vessel round the seaboard of Asia
Minor, intent on reaching Byzantium and the great
Egnatian Way.   For the life of Asia lies round its coasts.
Here the cities famous in Greek history are busy as ever:
Ephesus, Smyrna, Miletus, Pergamum are the chief.
Miletus exports the fine wools and woollens, blankets,
cloaks and carpets which are the produce of the sheep
which graze in the rich river-valleys near the coast.
From this region, too, come wine and oil in abundance
and dried fruits; Ephesus, too, is noted for its oysters,
and a variety of fish comes from the Troad; and from
the hinterland certain quantities of most of the minerals
under the sun.   Leaving the port of Seleucia we sail
up the coast, leaving Cyprus, where most of the copper
comes from, on the port bow.   Soon we are passing
the mouth of the Cydnus, up which Cleopatra sailed
with silver oars and purple sails to meet Antony at
Tarsus (a town also known to history as the birthplace
of Saint Paul, a university town where the young men
of Cilicia went to learn the rhetoric and philosophy
whose traces may be found in the Epistles of our New
Testament).   So on as the skipper of Saint Paul's boat
perhaps meant to go before he was driven from his course.

We are more fortunate and soon put into the fine harbour of Rhodes.   We proceed, threading the island channels of the much-indented coast, finding everywhere Greek cities with temples and thronged market-places and a twitter of many tongues with the insistent accents of Greek overriding all.   The old vitalities may have receded from the towns of the Greek mainland, but here on the Asiatic coast they are still in full tide.   And now we are off the Troad with the site of Troy away on our right, threading the Dardanelles narrows into the Sea of Marmora, bound for the Golden Horn.

Beyond the Strait of Byzantium lies a different world, where the bright turquoise of the Aegean gives place to the darker waters of the Black Sea, and on the shores are the pines and firs of the North.   On the farther shore away to the north begin the rich steppes of South Russia, rich in grain, whose trade at the moment is controlled by the little kingdom of Bosporus centring round the Crimea.   Beyond Bosporus are the roving tribes of the North, one day to give trouble to the frontier of the Empire, but not yet.   We do not go farther north in our tour than Byzantium, the Greek city so admirably situated to control the approaches to the Black Sea and therefore a noted port, but at the moment enjoying only a fraction of the significance which it is to have once the Emperor Constantine has turned it into Constantinople, the capital of the Eastern half of the Empire.   Along the via Egnatia a steady journey brings the traveller to Rome in twenty-four days.

So much for the East.   In this half of the world the seed of Rome fell on ground worked for centuries by earlier civilizations and did not take root and multiply as it did in the virgin West.   But it flourished under the

Roman peace and contributed its fair quota to the life
and wealth of the Empire.

We turn to the West. But first, to the south, there is
Roman Africa. We embark at Puteoli, in the Bay of
Naples, and in four days we are in Carthage on the other
shore of the Mediterranean. Fear of another Hannibal
and of a repetition of the Punic Wars had led Rome in
the middle of the second century B.C. to destroy this city;
but now that the threat was no more Carthage was too
good a harbour to be left unused, and it had been
restored. Here now were shipped the great grain-
cargoes and the fruit and vegetables from the excep-
tionally fertile North African soil. There were crafts,
too, in Carthage, glass-blowing and the dyeing of fabrics,
the making of textiles and pottery. Other prominent
products were salt from the inland lakes, horses and
sheep and the much-prized Numidian marble. The
Roman province of Africa was a quiet one, and the one
legion which was all that was necessary to ensure its
quiet (the legion III Augusta) must have had the most
peaceful regimental history ever known. Today the
noble ruins of Timgad bear witness to the civilizing
power of Roman forms in a land which had had little
history before the coming of Rome. Before the end of
the Western Empire Africa had given some notable
figures to the world of letters: Fronto, Aulus Gellius,
Apuleius the novelist, the Christian writers Tertullian
and Augustine of Hippo were all products of Roman
Africa. Once Claudius had added Morocco, Roman
Africa stretched peacefully from the Atlantic to the Nile,
a broad strip of prosperous country securely protected
on the south by the great Saharan desert.

Gaul, too, was a land which grew to great and lasting

prosperity under Rome. The coast-road from Italy through Liguria and what is now the Riviera is one of the busiest in the Empire. But the best approach is by sea from Ostia to Marseilles. Southern Gaul (Gallia Narbonensis) was Romanized so early that it came to be called *the* Province (" it is more like Italy than a province," says Pliny) and the name (Provence) has survived into modern times. Here the traveller will find flourishing towns and miles of warm hill-sides thickly cultivated with olive and vine. There are good harbours at Narbo, Arelate (Arles) and Forum Iulii (Fréjus), and at Arles are the potteries which are to flood Italian markets and others with their mass-produced bright red household ware.

North of Narbonensis, Gaul is a sterner land which bred good soldiers and the best cavalry in the Empire. Left to themselves these high-spirited tribes wasted their strength in tribal wars; Rome constrained them to peace. It is a land of great rivers, forests and rolling fertile plains. The rivers made communications easy, and under the Empire much of the trade traffic went by water. The forests bred the droves of swine which sent Rome hams and sausages and pickled meats; on the downlands Gallic sheep produced a thick wool, not so fine as that of Miletus but of excellent warmth; on the plains were the cattle and in some regions, especially to the west, corn was grown. And Pliny tells of geese driven all the way from Belgium down to the south to provide the ancient *pâté de foie gras* for the gourmets of Italy. In the towns the Gauls became expert crafts-men in glassware, pottery and textiles, in which they were soon capturing world markets. Augustus made new arterial roads, radiating from the central town of

Lugdunum (Lyons): one down the Rhone valley to Marseilles (where it met the highroad running east and west along the coast); one running north by the Seine to the shores of the Channel; one up to the legionary camps on the Rhine; one across the Jura and the Alps to Italy. Good paved roads ran over the Alpine passes, the Great and Little St. Bernards and the Mont Genèvre. With these secure links with Italy, Gaul entered on a long and prosperous life, taking the impress of Roman civilization very deep and giving Rome many distinguished figures, among whom we may pick out Agricola, the conqueror of Northern Britain, the Emperor Antoninus Pius and, in the late afternoon of Roman power, the poet Ausonius.

From Marseilles the via Domitia brings us through Arles and Nîmes (famous for its triple-arched aqueduct) into Spain. Here, too, was a rich land, not so much in the plantations (vines, olives and other fruits) which clothe the coast-lands of the south and the southern valleys as in the mineral wealth of the mountain-regions, especially down on the southern sierras and in the north-west. Spain gave Rome silver and gold, iron, copper, tin, lead, quicksilver and mica. The wealth of the south was legendary; here legend had set the garden of the Hesperides and the fields of the Blessed, where wondrous golden apples grew and horses, it was said, fed from silver mangers. In this fair southern land grazed strange black-fleeced sheep which gave wool of a unique quality, and the milk of the cows was so creamy that it had to be watered down before it could be made into cheese. And its wine and oil were exported in the great jars whose fragments can still be found behind the wharves of the Tiber (the well-known " Monte Testaccio," an artificial mound over one hundred feet high and half a mile round, was originally a dump of such fragments which grew up in the first and second centuries A.D.).

Because of the mountains Spain had been the hardest province of the Empire to master, but the mountain minerals made it worth mastering. The roads which established Roman control over the peninsula were a remarkable witness of Roman persistence and skill. As well as the via Domitia at the east end, there is a road over the Central Pyrenees to Saragossa (which is' what the name Caesaraugusta has become) and a road in the west by Roncevaux (where Roland died) to Pampeluna. Then there was the old coast-road from Tarraco (Tarragona, the old imperial capital) through Valentia to New Carthage, and that by way of Corduba and Hispalis (Seville) to Gades (Cadiz) on the other side of the Atlantic Strait. Dominating the new roads were new Roman cities: Asturica Augusta in the north-west, Caesaraugusta on the Ebro, the nobly-terraced Tarraco on the east coast, Emerita Augusta (Merida) on the Guadiana, Italica in the Guadalquivir country. Full use was made of such rivers as were navigable, and communications in general were good and quick: Tarraco was four days from Rome for any sizable craft; the passage from Gades to Ostia, we are told, could be made in seven days. Spain was so rich in natural products that she never developed the manufacturing industries of Gaul, but her towns became large and civilized and there are great names among the Spaniards of the Empire: Seneca and Lucan were of Spanish blood; so were Martial and Columella, and the great writer on education, Quintilian; and, among the Emperors, Spain could claim figures as great as Trajan and Hadrian.

Away to the north, on the shores of the Channel and the Rhine, loomed the unknown. Britain had faded out of the political picture since Julius Caesar's invasions and a century was to elapse before Rome set official foot in Britain again, but in the age of Augustus Britain was at peace under the domination of the big southern kingdom of Cunobelinus (Shakespeare's Cymbeline), and there was regular traffic over the Channel—hides, fleeces from the downs, lead and tin from the west, hunting-dogs and slaves. And a Roman tourist sailing from Boulogne and landing at Richborough or Deal might, if he could endure the humours of the strange tidal sea, under the escort of merchant friends have a fair glimpse of the green land which was one day to be Rome's. But he would be conscious of being very near the ends of the earth and would hear strange stories of northern seas still more remote, where mists were so thick that one could not distinguish sea from air and sky and of lands where the sun was known to shine at midnight.

Over the Rhine to the east was a more treacherous unknown. For in Germany proper, a difficult terrain for the soldier with its forests and swamps, the Roman never made himself at home; the annihilation of three whole legions there in A.D. 9 was a shock which Rome never forgot, and much experiment was needed before a satisfactory frontier was drawn along the linked lines of the Rhine and Danube. Over the Rhine at this time our traveller would not be likely to set foot, but farther south between North Italy and the Danube was a land he could still explore. He could find passable roads through Switzerland, once the work of pacifying the mountain tribes had been done by the stepson of Augustus. There was the road which from Milan round

Lake Como climbed over the Raetian Alps and led to Augsburg (Augusta Vindelicorum). There was another road to Augsburg from Verona up the valley of the Athesis farther to the east. Raetia was a land rich in timber, and there was a regular demand for its maple and larch down in the south; and early in the century Augsburg became a prosperous town where cattle-dealers rubbed shoulders with wool-merchants and dealers in hides. Nor must we forget the mineral wealth of the Alpine lands. Noricum exported iron to Italy, partly in the raw, partly worked up into knives and similar articles. In Noricum, too, as in Dalmatia, there were silver and gold to be mined. For the export of these products from the Danube lands the great *entrepôt* was Aquileia, the gate for all land-communications between Italy and the provinces of the Balkan hinterland. Aquileia was the southern end of the ancient Amber Route which since prehistoric times had brought amber from the Baltic to the civilized peoples of the south. Linked with Rome by means of the via Flaminia, it was also the meeting-place of all the roads which led through the eastern Alps to serve the provinces which Rome, at the beginning of the first century, was compacting on the southern shore of the Danube. At that time these lands had recognized possibilities, the metals of Noricum and Pannonia, wine and oil from certain parts of the gaunt land of Illyria, the rich corn-lands and pastures of Moesia, but it was not till the end of the century that they reached their great prosperity and moved Rome to step over the Danube and take in Dacia and so draw her final northern boundary round the country which today is called Roumania (" the Roman land ").

EPILOGUE

His ego nec metas rerum nec tempora pono;
imperium sine fine dedi.—VIRGIL.

" These have I set no bound in time or space; I have given them empire without end."

AUGUSTUS died in A.D. 14. In the forty-four years of his reign he reshaped the Roman world and reorganized the Roman State to ensure the peace he had made. His work endured. For long Rome kept the world at peace, teaching, as Virgil had claimed she should, law and government to the nations. There were wars, but, compared with the wars of the Republic, they were few and on the fringe; there were civil upheavals, but none of great consequence during the first two centuries A.D. Even the terrible year of the Four Emperors, A.D. 68–9, during which the generals of three armies fought for the throne vacated by the fallen Nero, left little imprint on the century that followed. Indeed, it was followed by the longest period of peace and prosperity that ancient Rome enjoyed: the age of Trajan, Hadrian and the Antonines.

During these two centuries we find the monarchy so carefully veiled by Augustus becoming an obvious and absolute despotism. Some of his successors lacked the will and some the skill to dissimulate; some were frankly anxious to assert tyrannical power. Tiberius was a misfit, Gaius a vicious experimenter in despotism on the Oriental model, Claudius a well-meaning but fussy reformer, Nero a vain dilettante tyrant; but, with all these vagaries at the Court, the life of the Empire continued imperturbably on its way. The Augustan machine stood the test. Nero's fall was the signal for civil war, but the triumphant competitor, Vespasian, proved a strong ruler and was succeeded peacefully by his two sons, Titus and Domitian, one after the other. Domitian, after a competent but unpopular rule, was assassinated, to give place to Nerva, the Senate's choice. With Nerva the dynastic idea which had so far dominated the succession was suspended. The next four Emperors owed their accession to adoption; that is to say, they were chosen by their predecessors as the right men for the throne and not for their family connections. Nerva ruled barely two years, but he adopted Trajan; Trajan adopted Hadrian; Hadrian adopted Antoninus; Antoninus adopted Marcus Aurelius. They were diverse characters, these four: Trajan was a soldier, caring for practicalities, competent, shrewd, incisive; Hadrian a wonderfully versatile and indefatigable patron, anxious, ubiquitous, caring for culture and the things of the mind, a Hellenist and a modernist at once; Antoninus, by way of contrast, was a calm aristocrat reassuring the world by the impassivity of his gaze on the Roman tradition, stressing continuity with the Roman past; Aurelius was an ascetic and a philosopher, a strange blend of Roman duties and Christian-like sensibilities. All were able rulers of a flourishing Empire.

With the accession of Aurelius's son Commodus the spell was broken, and the lean years came. For the next century a succession of short-lived Emperors appeared, set up and overthrown by force of arms. It was not till 284 that once more a strong ruler emerged to re-establish the discipline of the Empire. That was

Diocletian.   His task accomplished, in 304 he abdicated.
It was only after some seven years of civil war that the
next strong Emperor, Constantine, established himself.
Constantine did two things which were to have a pro-
found significance.   He made Christianity the religion
of the Empire and he built the city of Constantinople,
which foreshadowed the division of the Empire into two
halves, Eastern and Western.   He ruled from A.D. 311
to 337, and after his death a further age of divided
loyalties and disharmony began, to continue to the end
of the Western half of the Empire.

The great age of Rome was the first two centuries
A.D.   During that time Roman government, Roman
culture, Roman law fulfilled their mission in the world.
Compared with this period, the rest of the story is a
story of decline.   In proportion as the hold of the
central government on the Empire within grew weaker
in the age of military unrest, the Empire found it
increasingly difficult to resist the pressure on its frontiers
from the barbarian invaders without.   Far off in the
north and in the north-east, among the tribes of Russia
and the Central Steppes, mysterious forces, the " Wandering of the Peoples," had set in motion hordes of
barbarian humanity.   They came surging to the west
and the south, forcing other tribes to move on in front
of them.   The result was a continual pressure on the
north frontier of the Empire, varying in intensity and
direction, but a persisting and increasing menace.   The
first serious threats came on the Danube front towards
the end of the second century A.D. and were successfully countered.   In places Rome sought to solve the
problem by allowing barbarian tribes to settle inside
the boundaries of Empire.   This policy, conciliatory
16

and liberal though it may seem, proved in the long run disastrous. As it was extended, large sections of the Empire came to be dominated by a new, vigorous, barbarian stock; superficially Romanized barbarians found their way to high imperial office (such a one was Alaric the Goth, the Roman officer who came to be a sacker of Rome). Thus the inroads of barbarians from without were reinforced by the growth of barbarism within.

Towards the middle of the third century came the Alemanni (the French still call the Germans *allemands*), the Goths and then the Franks. In the same century the Picts and Scots from the north and the Saxon raiders from the east began to attack Britain. About the beginning of the fifth century the Vandals appear, and about 450 a terrible and cruel people called the Huns swept down on Southern Europe. In the incessant strain of resisting these invaders the vitality and resources of the Empire slowly ebbed. In the year 476 Augustulus, the last Emperor of the West, was deposed, and by the turn of the century the western provinces had become so many barbarian kingdoms. There were Gothic kingdoms in Italy and Spain, and a Vandal kingdom in Africa; the Franks were in the Gaul to which they were to give the name by which we know it; Roman Britain had become Saxon England. The great Roman Empire had passed away and the Dark Ages had set in, but from its fragments were to be forged the nations and cultures of modern Europe. In Italy, Gaul and Spain the Latin language lived on, to become the Italian, French and Spanish that we know. And the once-despised Christianity that Rome had embraced in the days of her decline saved, by converting the barbarian conquerors, much of the ancient wisdom which Rome had laboured to preserve.

In the East the other half of the Empire, round its capital, Constantinople, went on, and the Byzantine civilization came to full flower, reaching a brilliant peak in the reign of Justinian (527–565). His reign is famous not only for the great and final codification of Roman Law which goes by his name and for the building of the great church of Santa Sophia (" The Holy Wisdom "), but for a remarkable territorial recovery. In that reign Justinian's great general Belisarius drove off the attacking Bulgars and Lombards and reconquered for the Empire Vandal Africa and Gothic Italy, which for two centuries was a dominion of the Eastern Empire. At the end of the sixth century the coming of Islam brought a new menace. The Mohammedan Arabs overran Mesopotamia (where they set up the legendary Empire of Baghdad), the north coast of Africa and penetrated thence into Spain. In the course of this expansion the Empire suffered greatly, and Constantinople itself was besieged. Constantly weakened by the attacks of barbarian hordes, Bulgarians, Russians, Normans, it dwindled till there was little left but Constantinople and its immediate neighbourhood. Under its Emperors, who kept up Courts and hierarchies of an Oriental type, it lived on, the relic of a great past but still doing to civilized Europe the inestimable service of preserving the books and the knowledge of the great writers of Greek antiquity.

In the middle of the eleventh century the coming of the Turks and their conquest of Asia Minor and the Holy Land brought on the Crusades, which brought to the dying Empire a brief new lease of life in the

Crusaders' Latin kingdom of Constantinople. At the beginning of the fourteenth century the final enemies, the Ottoman Turks, appeared on the scene. For a long time the counter-threat of the Mongols kept them off. But in 1453 they captured Constantinople, and the Roman Empire was at last at an end. How the refugee scholars from the stricken city brought to an expectant Europe the treasures of Greek science and literature which for a thousand years had been lost to the Western world and so helped on the great movement which we call the Rebirth is an exhilarating story which we cannot pursue here. To the end Rome and its Empire had kept the ancient culture and transmitted it. It was this recovery of Greek and Greek science which made possible the open Bible in our Churches and the brilliant progress of modern science.

Such, in its last stages, is the story of Rome. Unfortunately it has been overlaid by an excessive readiness on the part of historians to find the whole story one of decline. Since the publication of Gibbon's classic work it has been hard to think of the Roman Empire except in terms of " Decline and Fall."

" Decline and Fall " has been a favourite heading with historians ever since the modern world undertook to chronicle the history of the ancient. It is more than a heading; it is an attitude. Gibbon first popularized it, and the phrase enjoyed a steady prosperity until the archaeologists towards the end of the last century began to redress the balance by calling in more concrete evidence than the moralizings of philosophers. Here, as in other fields, ancient history owes a great debt to Mommsen. But the old attitude has been long in dying

and is not yet dead. Gibbon in envisaging the whole
history of the Roman Empire from the settlement of
Augustus to the coming of the Ottomans was no doubt
justified in using the title he did. But his manner left
no doubt that even in the days of her first princeps
Rome was declining and falling hard.

The modern apologist, working in the light of modern
knowledge, will stress rather the merit of the imperial
achievement as compared with the republican; he will
show the B.C. centuries of Rome as a prologue to her
real work, the story of a state putting her own house
in order before setting out to govern the world; a period
in which Rome is not yet conscious of her mission. The
Gibbonite may object that Rome never did put her
house in order and point to Tacitus and Suetonius to
support the objection. About Tacitus and Suetonius
something will be said later ; to the objection itself we
may reply that it is based on the very fallacy which
cost republican Rome a century of civil war—the refusal
to distinguish between Rome the city-state and Rome
the world-empire, between parochial and civic virtues.
Even if the utter decadence of the city in the first century
A.D. could be proved, such a charge would have little
bearing upon the work of Rome as empire-builder and
civilizer.

And yet an inveterate air of pessimism, which even the
archaeologists have not dispelled for us, surrounds the
general study of Roman history. This pessimism grows
apace the farther we advance into the imperial era, but
it is not absent from the republican. We read of a
nation that gained the whole world and lost its soul in
the process, that was borne from strength to strength
(*moribus antiquis stat res Romana virisque*) by a sterling

character which somehow disintegrated before the course was run, whose religion and literature alike were choked and corrupted by insidious Greek influences. One writer gloomily chronicles the first divorce case in 231 B.C. as the beginning of the end, speedily followed by the first sumptuary law in 215 and the *senatus consultum de Bacchanalibus* of 186. Warde Fowler can write magisterially for all his gentleness, " In the second century B.C. the Roman was fast becoming spiritually destitute, without consolation, and without the sense that he needed it." At least we can congratulate the Roman on his innocence (the consolation which these *vaticinia post eventum* so charitably offer). Even when we come to the Rome of Augustus (*deus nobis haec otia fecit*) the pessimists are still with us; the Golden Age is, after all, it seems, but a red sunset, a Twilight of the world-conquerors. Professor Adcock in the tenth volume of the *Cambridge Ancient History* becomes cautiously elegiac as he sums up his own summary of a 500-page survey of the Augustan Age: " its temptation was to be static in high matters, political thought withered, so that the Empire lost the spirit of a common adventure, the welcome for what was new, without which the strongest and shrewdest political system is doomed in the end to become mechanical and sterile." Professor M. Lot, looking back over the history of Rome from the fourth century A.D. writes: " Ten centuries of corruption and three of despotism had brought the old society to a state of moral and material destitution." But Rome has a way of giving the lie to such academic wisdom. Despite all the prophets of doom the *res Romana* still goes on. She did not last for ever; but from Augustus to Augustulus is a long cry, and why give the impression that one might have confused the two ? If these things are said of the green tree, what shall be said of the dry ? Merely that it is an unconscionable time dying ?

We have already seen something of the misguidedness which has led writers to see in Roman history the story of a moral decline. It depends on the assumption that Rome as a tiny city-state started on her course adorned with all the virtues which the aristocratic propagandists claimed for her. As we have seen, this attractive picture, valuable and dynamic as an ideal, was as far as history goes largely a pious myth. Morality in the large sense was a thing which Rome achieved as she grew, not a Garden of Eden from which her destiny expelled her or a state of innocence from which she fell.

Morality apart, what reasons can be found for this general attitude to imperial Rome ? Various hints of explanation suggest themselves. First there is the consideration that Rome is nearer to us in time and other affinities than Greece; there is a continuity between our history and hers, between Roman culture and ours, a continuity which remains best illustrated in language. The reason why so strange and compelling a sense of freshness comes to us, " like a health-bringing wind blowing from a wholesome country," when we read an Aeschylean choric ode or a chapter of Thucydides, is not merely that these are the products of singularly healthy and alert minds but that the words in which they are written come to us with no sordid or petty associations. They are words which make us think of Simonides and Sappho, of Sophocles and Plato. They are the voice of an age brief and compact, which is perfect because it is dead, carved with a statuesque serenity, a classic frieze against the background of time. It is dead, and modern

Greek is a mere ghost of it. But with Rome it is different. The words of a Roman author do not enjoy, or only to a limited degree, that purity of appeal. Latin lasted so long that it is difficult to think of it as dead. It is a Tithonus among languages. It lived on to the fifteenth century in decrepitude and at the Renaissance was rejuvenated, but into a youth that was almost entirely academic. At the present time it is certainly a dead language, yet it lacks the canonized sanctity, the embalmed perfection of Greek. It has lived on to reach the threshold of the modern world, and, looking back, as yet we lack perspective. A little more distance, and enchantment may come. Perhaps we may connect with this a not dissimilar consideration. We are all familiar with the phenomenon of the exultation of the herd over the greatly fallen, over a Sejanus or a Wolsey; it is exemplified in the lives of actresses and cinema stars, boxers and athletes (" I see Wells has been knocked out by Carpentier again; well, he never *was* much of a boxer "). Is there some such element engrained in the vulgar attitude towards the Roman Empire as a great one that broke a world's record and then crashed ?

But when we come to major considerations it will be seen that those already advanced are on the fringe of the subject and are incapable of concrete demonstration. To any but the most casual reflection it is obvious that the Decline and Fall attitude is the result of a certain unfavourable estimate of the social and moral tone of the imperial age. Whence is this estimate derived ? Obviously from contemporary ancient writers. If we examine the extant literature of imperial Rome the general impression of Roman society received is inevitably unfavourable. The great names are with a few

exceptions the names of writers who were opposed either
to particular Emperors or to the imperial system. There is
little correspondingly on the credit side after Virgil and,
if there is, there is also a Gresham's law of traditions as of
money. Bad report drives out good. Even Virgil comes
to be discounted; "he was a bought propagandist."
Livy's Preface makes it clear that, however useful the
new peace in which he had leisure to write a history in
142 books, the good days of Rome were the good old
days of the Republic. This *laudatio temporis acti* is clear
enough in Juvenal and Tacitus too, though it is overshadowed by the tremendousness of the hatred which was
their driving force. Both, though they think it politic to
flatter the reigning Emperor, belong to the old conservative school, which was convinced that Rome was
going to the dogs, and collect all symptoms that can be
detected with an eagerness that bespeaks a partisan
prejudice rather than an honest concern. The Stoic
school was no more optimistic of the Rome of its day,
and the Stoic tradition falls into step beside the die-hard.
Even under the best administrations these dogs would
bark, as Vespasian remarked, and, though it was all
bark and no bite, had to be firmly muzzled. And perhaps Suetonius, that most short-sighted of pedagogues,
has the most to answer for. It is left to a few provincials
to lift up the honest voice of praise over the good work
of Rome. But who reads a Claudian and a Rutilius
to-day? Then with the growing of a Christian literature the scales of judgement are loaded against Rome
once and for all.

The mention of Christianity brings us to the most
important consideration of all. If there is any one self-
sufficient explanation of our attitude it is here. Between

the Christian and Roman ideals of the early centuries A.D. there is a disjunction which is perfect. Rome stands for corporate civic strength, Christianity (at least in its early stages when the Second Advent was a daily possibility) abominates all that is secular; Rome stands for a disciplined society in which tolerance allows all sorts to live together in peace, Christianity is a narrowly exclusive sect which shrinks apart. When Rome was doing all she could to hold together society and civilization, Christianity was becoming chief of the forces of disintegration. In the end Christianity triumphed, but who shall say that its enemy was Rome? No doubt it shed (as unfeelingly as any fledgeling) the shell which had fostered it; but the shell had been cracked from outside. Now it is a momentous happening that the beginnings of the Christian and the Roman imperial eras nearly coincide in time. The two were enemies from birth. The Roman Empire is dead, the Christian Church lives on. The Empire began in pride and splendour, the Church in humility and insignificance. What is more tempting than to conclude that the Empire right from the beginning weakened in proportion as the Church grew strong? that this is the supreme application of the Gospel words " He that would save his soul, the same shall lose it " ? that the coincidence in time was the calculated ordinance of a didactic providence?

It was left for the life of one Roman Emperor to point the moral and conviction was complete. There is indeed a curious irony in the story of Marcus Aurelius, the philosopher-king who was the first of a series of good rulers to abandon, in favour of a worthless son, the philosophical principle of succession by adoption, and was also the saint who persecuted Christianity.

Further, though his heart was set on the things of the spirit, he was forced by circumstance to spend his reign in war. In his reign the Empire shows the first signs of territorial dissolution, hints of a crumbling at the edges; nothing very much, but how significant to the historian who has taken on himself the role of a prophet of doom. It is hard not to sentimentalize over Aurelius, hard to achieve a reasonable estimate of him. The counter-attractions of Christian sentiment and the historian's wisdom-after-the-event distort the view from either side. But as a healthy ruler of a prosperous state Aurelius can never be reclaimed. He is condemned to wander down the corridors of history a lost soul, the Gentile who heard the Call but lacked the faith to abandon the Mammon of Rome; " for he was one that had great possessions." We may plead for the substitution of " responsibilities " for " possessions " in the indictment, but early Christianity would not admit the plea. There were no possessions but in Heaven, and the fabric of the *pax Romana* was as susceptible to moth and rust as more mundane garments, and when it crumbled Christianity, a more practical and helpful Christianity by now, could rise and preach with the greater effect.

We know now the debt which both Christianity and the modern Western civilization at large owe to the work of imperial Rome. Our history books are no longer variations on conservative and prejudiced themes. We are beginning to appreciate something of what the *res Romana* did for such countries as Spain and Gaul. But when we come to sum up we tend to hark back to the traditional mode. A little learning is a dangerous thing, and the ignorant will always preach where the wise inquire. How many estimates of republican society, much less of imperial, are free of this heavy bias ? Why not admit that in most departments the changes in republican society from those parochial beginnings were for the better, for the benefit of the world to be ? After all, the new standards of living brought more than mere extravagance and luxury; they brought taste and culture and a deeper intellectualism. If " morality " declined, humanity grew and spread. The old narrow-mindedness was tempered by a new breadth of outlook which fitted Rome for her great responsibilities. No doubt there were many blunders and lapses and failures, but could experiments on so vast a scale be expected without them ? During the first two centuries A.D. for every decadent among the nobility of fashionable Rome there must have been a hundred or a thousand nameless ones, proud of a new privilege, proud of Rome, working for her in the cause of civilization, making law, society, roads, towns, government, peace. For them the name of Rome assumed the proportions of a gospel. No doubt the worship of *dea Roma* was misguided in that it elevated a means into an end; but after all its fruits were secular, not spiritual, and the material it served to inspire is too widely bound up with our Western life to be ignored. In the third and fourth centuries even provincial spirit decayed, duties and obligations were avoided; bureaucracy resulted in standardization and paralysis. The decay is manifest and its causes, economic and otherwise, are not far to seek; but it is fatally easy to read the seeds of decay in the beginning, to over-emphasize the rigidity and lifelessness of the Roman machine. If Rome had been " ruining herself for six centuries," her legacy to the world is all the more remarkable.

BOOK LIST

NOTE.—*This is a select list of works which give fuller information on various aspects of the Roman world.*

GENERAL

ed. C. Bailey: *The Legacy of Rome* (Oxford, 1923).

(Essays by expert writers on the various aspects of the Roman civilization: Government, Law, Philosophy, Architecture, Language, etc.)

W. Warde Fowler: *Rome* (Home University Library, 1912).

T. R. Glover: *The Ancient World* (Cambridge U.P., 1935).

(An attractive, informal survey of the Greek, Roman and Jewish culture considered together and in relation to their background.)

W. C. Greene: *The Achievement of Rome* (Harvard U.P., 1933).

F. G. Moore: *The Roman's World* (Columbia U.P., 1936).

M. Rostovtzeff: *A History of the Ancient World*, Vol. II (Oxford, 1928).

(A clear and vigorous survey of Roman history, with a wealth of excellent photographs illustrating Roman life.)

T. Bossert & W. Zschietzschmann: *Hellas and Rome* (Zwemmer, 1936).

(A picture book.)

E. R. Bevan: *The World of Greece and Rome* (Benn, 1928).

(An excellent introduction in brief.)

ROMAN HISTORY

Among short histories the following may be recommended:

M. Cary: *History of Rome* (Macmillan, 1935).

C. E. Robinson: *A History of Rome* (Methuen, 1937).

G. H. Stevenson: *The Roman Empire* (Nelson, 1930).

M. P. Nilsson: *Imperial Rome* (Chatto and Windus, 1926).

For more detailed study there are:

The Cambridge Ancient History, Vols. VII–XII.

H. H. Scullard: *A History of the Roman World 753–146 B.C.* (Methuen, 1935).

F. B. Marsh: *A History of the Roman World 146–30 B.C.* (Methuen, 1935).

H. M. D. Parker: *A History of the Roman World 138–337 A.D.* (Methuen, 1935).

On the transition from Republic to Empire the following are valuable studies:

R. Syme: *The Roman Revolution* (Oxford, 1939).

F. B. Marsh: *The Founding of the Roman Empire* (Oxford, 1927).

Rice Holmes: *The Architect of the Roman Empire* (Oxford, 1931).

John Buchan: *Julius Caesar* (Peter Davies, 1932).

John Buchan: *Augustus* (Hodder and Stoughton, 1937).

For the end of the story may be recommended:

F. Lot: *The End of the Ancient World* (Kegan Paul, 1931).

H. St. L. B. Moss: *The Birth of the Middle Ages* (Oxford, 1935).

H. Pirenne : *Mohammed and Charlemagne* (Allen & Unwin, 1939).

THE ROMAN STATE

A. H. J. Greenidge: *Roman Public Life* (Macmillan, 1911).

G. H. Stevenson: *Roman Provincial Administration* (Blackwell, 1939).

J. Déclareuil: *Rome the Law-Giver* (Kegan Paul, 1927).

C. W. C. Oman: *Seven Roman Statesmen* (Arnold, 1911).

A. N. Sherwin-White : *The Roman Citizenship* (Oxford, 1939).

ROMAN LIFE AND SOCIETY

The British Museum Guide to the Exhibition illustrating Greek and Roman Life.

W. Warde Fowler: *Social Life at Rome in the Age of Cicero* (Macmillan, 1908).

T. G. Tucker: *Life in the Roman World of Nero and St. Paul* (Macmillan, 1910).

A. Gwynn: *Roman Education from Cicero to Quintilian* (Oxford, 1926).

Grant Showerman: *Rome and the Romans* (Macmillan Co., New York, 1931).

(Copious illustrations of Roman antiquities and landscape.)

R. H. Barrow: *Slavery in the Roman Empire* (Methuen, 1928).

A. M. Duff: *Freedmen in the Early Roman Empire* (Oxford, 1928).

R. C. Carrington: *Pompeii* (Oxford, 1936).

(Full of information about Roman houses, with good photographs.)

BOOK LIST 255

ROME AT WORK

Tenney Frank: *An Economic History of Rome* (Baltimore, 1927).
W. E. Heitland: *Agricola* (Cambridge U.P., 1921).
M. Rostovtzeff: *Social and Economic History of the Roman Empire* (Oxford, 1926).
   (Has many excellent illustrations.)
M. P. Charlesworth: *Five Men* (Oxford, 1936).
   (Portraits of imperial types: the Native Ruler, the Philosopher, the Adventurer, the Administrator, the Merchant.)
H. M. D. Parker: *The Roman Legions* (Oxford, 1928).
G. E. Cheesman: *The Auxilia of the Roman Army* (Oxford, 1914).
P. Louis: *Ancient Rome at Work* (New York, 1927).

ROMAN RELIGION

F. Altheim: *History of Roman Religion* (Methuen, 1937).
W. Warde Fowler: *Roman Ideas of Deity* (Macmillan, 1914).
W. Warde Fowler: *The Religious Experience of the Roman People* (Macmillan, 1911).
W. R. Halliday: *The Pagan Background of Early Christianity* (Univ. of Liverpool Press, 1925).
T. R. Glover: *The World of the New Testament* (Cambridge U.P., 1931).
T. R. Glover : *Conflict of Religions in the Early Roman Empire* (Cambridge, 1909).
L. R. Taylor: *The Divinity of the Roman Emperor* (New York, 1931)

HOLIDAYS AND ENTERTAINMENT

W. Warde Fowler: *The Roman Festivals* (Macmillan, 1908).
E. N. Gardiner: *Athletics of the Ancient World* (Oxford, 1930).
M. Bieber: *The History of the Greek and Roman Theater* (Princeton U.P., 1939).

SCIENCE, LETTERS AND ART

B. Farringdon: *Science in Antiquity* (Home University Library, 1938).
ed. C. Bailey: *The Mind of Rome* (Oxford, 1926).
   (Essays by various scholars on the different aspects of Roman Literature.)
J. Wight Duff: *A Literary History of Rome to the Close of the Golden Age* (Allen & Unwin, 1927).

J. Wight Duff: *A Literary History of Rome in the Silver Age* (Allen & Unwin, 1927).

Allen W. Seaby: *Art in the Life of Mankind*, Vol. II (Rome) (Batsford, 1931).

R. P. Hinks: *Greek and Roman Portrait Sculpture* (British Museum, 1935). (Has some excellent photographs.)

D. M. Robertson: *Handbook of Greek and Roman Architecture* (Cambridge U.P., 1929).

M. Cary and E. H. Warmington: *The Ancient Explorers* (Methuen, 1929).

GREATER ROME

M. P. Charlesworth: *Trade Routes of the Roman Empire* (Cambridge U.P., 1926).

J. Holland Rose: *The Mediterranean in the Ancient World* (Cambridge U.P., 1933).

R. G. Collingwood: *Roman Britain* (Oxford, 1923). (The best introductory work.)

R. G. Collingwood and J. L. N. Myres: *Roman Britain and the English Settlements* (Oxford History of England, Vol. I.; Oxford, 1936).

NOVELS

There is a rich variety of novels, varying in accuracy and depth, which give graphic accounts of life in the Roman world. The following may be recommended:

Naomi Mitchison: *The Conquered* (Cape, 1923). (A vivid picture of the Gaul conquered by Julius Caesar.)

Naomi Mitchison: *When the Bough Breaks* (Cape, 1924). (Stories of the Roman Empire: the Gaul of Caesar's time, the travels of Saint Paul, the Gothic invasions.)

Phyllis Bentley: *Freedom Farewell* (Gollancz, 1935). (A novel of the life of Julius Caesar.)

Jack Lindsay: *Rome for Sale* (Elkin Mathews & Marrot, 1934). *Caesar is Dead* (Nicholson & Watson, 1934). *Last Days with Cleopatra* (Nicholson & Watson, 1935). (A trilogy of the age of Revolution, the last century of the Republic.)

Jack Lindsay: *Despoiling Venus* (Nicholson & Watson, 1935).

W. G. Hardy: *Turn Back the River* (Lovat Dickson, 1936). (Pictures of Roman society life of the time of Cicero.)

Gertrude Atherton: *Golden Peacock* (Thornton Butterworth, 1937).
(Society in the Augustan age.)

G. Birkenfeld: *Augustus* (Constable, 1935).

H. Dupuy-Mazuel: *Lovers in Galilee* (Hurst & Blackett, 1934)⸴
(The sub-title is " An Idyll of the time of Tiberius.")

P. L. Anderson: *Pugnax the Gladiator* (Appleton-Century, 1939).
(Contains some vivid pictures of gladiatorial life.)

Robert Graves: *I, Claudius* (Barker, 1934).
Claudius the God (Barker, 1934).
(A remarkable combination of historical research and fiction which gives a graphic picture of life in the Court of the early Empire.)

N. Petersen: *The Street of the Sandal-makers* (Lovat Dickson, 1933).
(Life in Rome in the age of Marcus Aurelius.)

Walter Pater: *Marius the Epicurean* (Macmillan, 1885).
(A famous Victorian classic: a study of the religious atmosphere of Rome in the age of Aurelius.)

Robert Graves: *Count Belisarius* (Cassell, 1938).
(A novel of the age of Justinian.)

17

INDEX

A

abacus, 68
Abeona, 157
Actium, 174, 222
actors, 173
Adcock, Professor F. E., 246
Adeona, 157
Adriatic, 20, 21, 222
aediles, 36, 39–40
Aegean, 16, 224, 232
Aeneas, 60
Aequi, 19
Aeschylus, 197, 247
Aesculapius, 195, 197
Africa, 20, 22, 54, 103, 117, 162, 192, 233, 242, 243
Agatharchus, 195
Agricola, 84–5
Agrippa, 194
alae (army), 43–4
(architectural), 88 ff.
Alaric, 242
Aldwych farces, 171
Alemanni, 242
Alexander, 16, 114, 149, 191, 192, 193
Alexandria, 120, 179, 183, 191, 220, 224, 226–7, 230
algebra, 184
Alpine passes, 18, 235, 238
Ambarvalia, 153
amber route, 238
amphitheatre, 30, 164 ff.
Anaxagoras, 186
Anaximenes, 184
Antioch, 120, 230–1
Antonines, 239
Antoninus (Emperor)', 212, 235, 240
Antony, 65, 82, 227, 228
Apennines, 17
Apollo, 144, 149, 159, 222, 224
appeal, to Caesar, 49; to the Assembly, 55–7
Appian Way, 83, 217, 221
Appius Claudius, 200
Apuleius, 206, 233
aqueducts, 30, 206, 210, 235
Aquileia, 238

Ara Pacis, 211
Arabia, 225, 229
Arabs, 184, 243
arcade, 209
arches, 209, 218
Archimedes, 179, 183
architecture, 86 ff., 206 ff.
Arelate (Arles), 134
Argos, 223
Ariminum, 42
Aristarchus of Samos, 188
Aristophanes, 198
Aristotle, 185, 191, 227
arithmetic, 181
Armenia, 190
army, 24, 74, 109 ff.
Arno, River, 20
Arretium, 134
Arria, 65
Arsinoe, 225
arts, 206 ff.
Arval brethren, 143, 160
Asia, 22, 41, 220, 228 ff.
Asia Minor, 21, 76, 78, 145, 231 ff., 243
Assemblies, 35, 37 ff., 55
astronomy, 187
Asturica Augusta, 236
Atellane plays, 170
Athene, 16, 141
Athens, 16, 223, 224
athletics, 174–5
Atia, 67
Atlas Mountains, 190
atomic theory, 146, 185–6
atrium, 86 ff., 96
Attica, 223
Augsburg, 238
Augurs, 143
Augustine, Saint, 16, 117, 206, 233
Augustulus, 242, 246
Augustus, 25, 38, 41, 53, 67, 90 and passim
Aurelian, 210
Aurelius, *see* Marcus
Ausonius, 235
Auxiliaries, 111, 112, 117